BISON BOOKS

Appreciation:

Painting, Poetry and Prose

by Leo Stein

Introduction to the Bison Books Edition

by Brenda Wineapple

University of Nebraska Press
Lincoln and London

Manufactured in the United States of America

♾ The paper in this book meets the minimum requirements of American National Standard for Information Sciences—Permanence of Paper for Printed Library Materials, ANSI Z39.48-1984.

First Bison Books printing: 1996
Most recent printing indicated by the last digit below:
10 9 8 7 6 5 4 3 2 1

Library of Congress Cataloging-in-Publication Data
Stein, Leo, 1872–1947.
Appreciation: painting, poetry and prose / by Leo Stein; introduction to the Bison Books edition by Brenda Wineapple.
p. cm.
Originally published: New York: Crown Publishers, 1947.
Includes bibliographical references and index.
ISBN 0-8032-9236-8 (pbk.: alk. paper)
1. Literature—History and criticism. 2. Art. I. Title.
PN37.S75 1996
809′.93357—dc20
95-41855 CIP

Reprinted from the original 1947 edition by Crown Publishers, New York. Published by arrangement with Crown Publishers, Inc. This Bison Books edition follows the original in beginning the foreword on arabic page 7; no material has been omitted.

To Beatrice and Fred Stein

Introduction to the Bison Books Edition

Brenda Wineapple

In the five decades since his death in 1947, Leo Stein has been lampooned, pilloried, and otherwise ignored in book after book about his illustrious sister Gertrude. Caricature and foil, he appears as the lanky older brother, the stentorian one who holds court, his gold-rimmed spectacles aglow, as he gestures toward the brazen canvases—perhaps Matisse's extraordinary *Le Bonheur de Vivre* or Picasso's *Three Women*—that hung from floor to ceiling of 27, rue de Fleurus. Gertrude, meanwhile, sits in the background silent and seething. She is waiting for the right moment to fling off the paternal yoke, depose her brother, and declare herself the solitary genius of their shared household. Once she does, she will become the literary maverick, par excellence, of the twentieth century.

Like all stories, this one contains a degree of truth. But to the extent that it's culled from Gertrude Stein's charming memoirs, such as *The Autobiography of Alice Toklas* or *Everybody's Autobiography*, it's necessarily partial and partisan, constructed from the rationalizations of a relationship that failed. And, moreover, because Gertrude Stein was in fact the unique, unclassifiable, and elusive agent of the modern, Leo Stein was per force disenfranchised—not just by his sister or her later supporters but by the politics of modernism itself, which takes no prisoners.

But in fact for almost ten years, from 1903 to 1913, Leo Stein was one of the first champions and propagandizers of modern painting. He became friends with Matisse in 1905, the year of the sensational Autumn Salon, where the painter was considered by critic Louis Vauxcelles to be one of the wildest of "Les Fauves." Leo carried a trophy from that exhibit, the scandalous *Woman with a Hat*; and by then he already owned the work of Cézanne, Renoir, Gauguin, Vallotton, and Manguin. Also in that same year, he met the impoverished, undiscovered Pablo Picasso, whose work he began to buy. "This was the real thing," Stein later reminisced about Picasso, long after he tired of both the artist and his work.

Art was Stein's passion. It was also the reason he had settled in Florence in 1900 at the age of twenty-eight, intending to write a book on the Renaissance painter André Mantegna. Discovering in Mantegna's form and color a path that led, he later said, directly to Cézanne, Leo Stein for a short intense period, according to Museum of Modern Art founder Alfred H. Barr Jr., became "possibly the most discerning connoisseur and collector of 20th-century painting in the world."[1]

Stein began collecting early. After an expenses-paid trip around the world in 1896 with a wealthy cousin, he had returned home with a cache of Japanese prints. Then in England in 1902, having given up Mantegna, he bought his first modern painting, a Wilson Steer. But it was Paris that made the difference. Arriving in late 1902, he rented an apartment and studio at 27, rue de Fleurus, hung his prints on the wall, and decided to become a painter. When not sketching in front of a life-model, he perused the galleries and official salons, always looking to buy more. Little, however, piqued his interest until Bernard Berenson suggested he try Ambroise Vollard's gallery on the Rue Lafitte. A few visits later, Leo purchased Cézanne's *Landscape with Spring House*; this event, more than any other, propelled him into the role for which he became best known: that of modern art's garrulous advocate and its perspicacious collector.

"I was a Columbus setting sail," Leo Stein recalls in *Appreciation*, "for the world beyond the world." The following summer Stein returned to Florence where he carefully studied the Cézannes owned by the American collector Charles Loeser; in Paris he continued to spend days at the Autumn Salon where, he says in these pages, he examined paintings just as a botanist might inspect the flora of an unknown land. The simile was intentional. Having earned a degree in biology at Johns Hopkins in 1898, he had started graduate work and, as he recounts, originally "thought of myself as essentially a scientist—one who tried to find out why and how things were, rather than to create or re-create them." Although he never became more than a desultory painter who intermittently produced mediocre canvases, he remained a tireless investigator bent on understanding why and how artists painted as they did. "The problem was to see," he notes in this volume, "and then to learn what was particular about this way of seeing."

He also loved what he saw and was particularly proud of his purchase of Cézanne's *Portrait of Madame Cézanne*, under which his sister Gertrude, then living with him at the rue de Fleurus, said she wrote her first published book, *Three Lives*. Two Gauguins, two Cézannes, a Toulouse-Lautrec, and two Renoirs later (financed with his and his sister's mutual funds as well as the money earned from the sale of several Japanese prints), Stein excitedly confided to a friend that he was beginning to comprehend "the vital art of today," and was now eager to purchase Manet, Vuillard, Degas, Bonnard, and Van Gogh.[2]

By the fall of 1905, Leo and Gertrude Stein had laid the foundation of their collection, adding not just the celebrated *Woman with the Hat,* but two paintings by the young hard-up Picasso, *The Acrobat's Family with a Monkey* and *Young Girl with Basket of Flowers.* Word spread quickly, with so many clamoring to see the canvases that the Steins opened their atelier on Saturday nights. "People came," Leo Stein writes in *Appreciation*, "and so I explained, because it was my nature to explain." Although some grumbled, annoyed both by the pictures and what they called Stein's arrogance, preferring him to cater to their taste rather than instruct it, they continued to come and to listen. Even friends in America began to refer to the shared Stein studio as a salon: "I feel impelled to come over and see it. You must have some dandy things," said one. "Why don't we see some Renoirs and Cézannes over here?"[3]

Within this small compass, Leo Stein flourished; he was, in a sense, its center. He introduced artists to one another and to pictures they'd never before dreamed of; for many, it was their first glimpse of Cézanne, Matisse, and Picasso. Stein loaned paintings, money, time, and criticism. He inspired, cajoled, boosted. He was opinionated, lively, genuinely curious, and intelligent. If his manner seemed affected, his enthusiasm was unfeigned and often prescient. Max Weber, Andrew Dasburg, Morgan Russell, Mahonri Young, Patrick Henry Bruce, Elie Nadelman, Edward Steichen, the collector Albert Barnes—all profited from Stein's zeal, and of course Henri Matisse and Pablo Picasso were its direct beneficiaries.

But when Leo Stein loudly disparaged cubism and began to sell off his discoveries, replacing them with more affable Renoirs, Stein alienated many of the artists he'd previously inspired. Cubism was an experiment, yes, said Stein, but ultimately trifling: its challenge to Renaissance perspective was overstated, its quest for the essence of form laughable. Programmatic and hyper-intellectualized, cubism substituted analysis for imagination; its so-called vitality derived only from Picasso's endless ingenuity, that was all.

Stein's criticisms were not as thick-headed as was later supposed. He did not cling to outmoded notions of representational realism; on the contrary, facile divisions between the representational and non-representational interested him little. He believed the best in art joined subject and object; cubism failed because it lost touch both with the object and the onlooker, degenerating into an artistic solipsism buoyed only by a theory.

Such was also, in a nutshell, his argument—at least the aesthetic version of it—with his prolific sister Gertrude. Sometimes her rhythms were nice, he conceded, and no one better understood human character, but by and large her portrait-writing was nonsense. When "the only nature the artist recognizes is his own," Leo Stein remarked in an essay later published in *The New Republic*, it augurs a cult of "self-expression" that severs ties with the human, social, and historical community.[4] Artists "specially obsessed by the superior validity of the abstract" didn't automatically make interesting or expressive pictures. "In the main," he concluded, "these pictures excited more conversation than they induced contemplation."[5]

Indeed, the endless conversations rocking prewar Paris exasperated the once-genial Leo Stein, who thought such cerebral discussion produced more manifestoes than good pictures. "Everybody can see how ridiculous are tweedledum's pretensions but believes that as tweedledee he has at last solved the almost insoluble problem of art," Stein commented to a friend in 1913.[6] He'd had enough. Increasingly isolated and decidedly out of fashion, he withdrew from the Paris art world, shunned the Saturday night salon and retired the following year to the small, picturesque Italian hill town of Settignano, not far from the Berensons' villa, "to grow cabbages and things in the classical style," he joked. "I am no longer a prophet in Israel or at best only a Jeremiah."[7]

Retirement may have been his goal, but silence was something else again. Yet every time he tried to put pen to paper, he fell ill.

In a sense, Leo Stein was his own worst enemy. A perfectionist frequently paralyzed by criticism, he limited himself to the most evanescent of all genres, talk. He rarely published his ideas. In fact, during a lifetime committed to art and aesthetics he wrote only two books, a thorny volume called *The A-B-C of Aesthetics*, which did not appear until he was fifty-five, and *Appreciation*, printed twenty years after that.

Born on 11 May 1872 in Allegheny, Pennsylvania, Leo Stein was the youngest son of Daniel and Amelia Stein, his German Jewish and somewhat peripatetic parents. There were five children in all, but Leo felt close only to his baby sister, Gertrude, two years his junior. They were constant companions, loving and loyal and growing accustomed, from an early age, to exile. The family had moved to Vienna when Leo was a toddler, then a few years later to Paris and on to Oakland, California, where the despotic Daniel Stein relentlessly pursued the American dream. But he died young, in January 1891, following his wife Amelia to the grave just two years after her own early death. Leo was an eighteen-year-old sophomore at Berkeley at the time. Underage, he and Gertrude became the wards of their somber, successful oldest brother Michael, who readily approved when Leo decided to leave for Harvard. Gertrude and their sister Bertha also headed east, bound for Baltimore, Maryland, to live with relatives until Gertrude could join Leo in Cambridge. Michael, remaining in San Francisco with their brother Simon, turned their father's dream of prosperity into a comfortable stipend; it supported all of them for most of their lives.

By all external standards, Leo was rather successful at Harvard. In less than two years, he was admitted into the Law School without having bothered about an undergraduate degree. His aptitude for law, however, was not matched by much enthusiasm. And although he gladly quit school, he returned to Cambridge after his world tour in the first evident throes of what would become a lifelong crisis of vocation or, in the parlance of the times, neurasthenia.

Neurasthenia was a catch-all term for the malaise afflicting sensitive young men uncertain about themselves, their masculinity, and their future. Unlike the stalwart persons of Leo's acquaintance who embraced the strenuous life, or said they did, the neurasthenic male felt out of place at the country club and uncomfortable in the venerable, established professions. Some articulated such discomfiture in political terms. Hutchins Hapgood, for example, whom Stein had met en route to Japan, found a niche at Lincoln Steffens's *Commercial Advertiser*, decrying the hypocrisy and brutality of American life. Leo, however, just wanted to study art.

But America was hard on men who fooled with fans and things. And so he took refuge in Italy. Notwithstanding, the inhibitions haunting him since childhood pursued him abroad, preventing him from doing what he wanted to do: write. He abandoned the Mantegna project as soon as he heard another was publishing on the same subject; gifted in the art of postponement, he was equally adept at rationalization. Thus, his first years in Paris were a respite of sort in which evasion proved creative. For early in 1903 he'd enrolled at the Julian Academy, always hospitable to foreigners, and there met many of the artists he soon encouraged. He wasn't much of a painter, but his peers admired his eloquence and his eye, which in these years was unerring.

His friends eagerly awaited a book. Alfred Stieglitz, Gertrude's first American publisher, told Leo he would print anything Leo wanted to write. Nothing came. Instead, together with his sister, Leo Stein created a private world at 27, rue de Fleurus that was open to the public. Herself having abandoned a career in medicine and now a fledgling author, Gertrude had joined Leo shortly after he'd settled in Paris, and during this time sister and brother were virtually inseparable, their lives entwined, their interests overlapping. But a smoldering rivalry seemed destined, at least in hindsight, to erupt and divide. For the last thirty years of their lives, they did not speak to one another. They differed irrevocably over Gertrude's writing; new loves entered each of their lives; and the ambitions that nurtured each of them sustained only one. That one was Gertrude.

Leo Stein's quarrel both with her work and with cubism antagonized those, like his sister and Picasso, destined for renown, and this accounts at least in part for his later image as a curmudgeonly philistine embittered by his sister's (and Picasso's) success. Such a view was reinforced in 1950 with the posthumous publication of a series of letters, journal entries, and autobiographical fragments, *Journey into the Self*, a volume that inadvertently damaged Stein's reputation even further. Individual letters were edited and selections generally made in conformity with 1950s standards of taste. As a consequence, much of Stein's pith is removed, his preoccupation with psychological issues not given ample context, his warmth and compassion all but excised, and his ongoing self-analysis robbed of its poignancy. All this is unfortunate, for it has worked to flatten the complexities of Leo Stein.

A man whose talk was considered the most remarkable of his generation and whose conversation nurtured some of the most important artists of the early twentieth century, Leo was erudite, passionate, often brilliant—a "some lesser Samuel Johnson driving a small wedge into the American mind by the force of his superior logic," art critic Jerome Mellquist wrote in the *New York Times* when reviewing *Appreciation*.[8] Stein's rejection of cubism (and his sister's writing) was sincere, and if its virulence was personally motivated, his argument remains animated and frank. He was not an easy man, nor a simple one.

In the United States during the First World War, Leo Stein plunged into psychoanalysis to overcome the debilitating writer's block he could no longer avoid. A frequent guest at Mabel Dodge's Fifth Avenue salon, he moved quietly in the New York intellectual circle that took him to the offices of *The Dial*, *Seven Arts*, and the recently founded *New Republic*, where he began to contribute art criticism and reviews, and by 1927, after he'd returned to Italy and married, he published *The A-B-C of Aesthetics* with Boni and Liveright.

His *New Republic* essays were light pieces that provided an introduction to the contentious, often witty host of the rue de Fleurus. Chafing against the grain, he was prickly and surprisingly mild-mannered; short-sighted and shrewd, he was frequently so radical he seemed reactionary—and vice versa. But it is easy to see how Stein was construed as hopelessly traditional, given his almost irrational animus against cubism. Though at times a fierce formalist, he also disavowed distinctions between high and low, good and bad; he thought the museum a necessary evil that could be usefully supplanted with the distribution of high-quality reproductions; he believed all pious discussions about Great Books or Great Ideas hopelessly small, especially those about the notion of the classics as a standard. "Standard of what, in Heaven's name? Standard of Deportment—only that and nothing more."[9] Indeed, he who dedicated his whole life to art believed that by and large art is overvalued and perhaps not even very important, except as part of a larger social enterprise. In that case, art, like science, can actually change people and the quality of their lives.

To that end, his *A-B-C of Aesthetics* was intended to offer a guide to seeing aesthetically, but it confounded most of its readers. Arguing that emotion has nothing to do with aesthetic enjoyment, that most criticism is nothing more than a form of gossip, and refusing to discuss particular objects of art, Stein eluded anyone looking for precise definitions or programs. A devotee of William James, his pragmatic allergy toward all-encompassing ideas cost the book much clarity. And its highly personal nature prompted one reviewer to suggest Stein wrote as if he was still discoursing over the marble-top of a Paris café, dazzling his listeners as he ranged over a wide field of related subjects but leaving his audience, in the end, breathless and perplexed. Horace Kallen, who found much to praise, called the book a marvelous soliloquy; so it was. But Stein was devastated. Again he lapsed into silence.

Twenty more years passed before Stein published another book. This was *Appreciation*. Begun just after the outbreak of the Second World War, Stein wrote it sporadically during the war years while he and his French wife lived on in a ravaged Italy. His share of the famed art collection was mostly gone. Food was scarce, the batteries on his hearing device had long since died, and Nina Stein earned a pittance by occasionally teaching English. Stein assumed his advanced age protected him from deportation or worse, but toward the end of the war, he and Nina were forced underground to hide in a dark cellar.

Yet twenty years of self-analysis had borne their fruit. Stein never abandoned his sense of humor, his compassion, or his skepticism. He weathered the poverty and anxiety of these last years with a measure of grace and a good deal of hope. For he was writing again with a verve that demonstrated once and for all Stein's unruly, often contrary originality. Even he seemed to know it. The result was the mercurial, accessible, and partly autobiographical *Appreciation: Painting, Poetry, and Prose*, a tour de force of wit, aperçu, and wisdom lightly worn. In a book that again addressed the major aesthetic issues preoccupying him for a lifetime—he called it a "little debauch in the realm of ideas"—Leo Stein had finally found his voice: intimate, wryly amusing, and above all true to his own captious vision.

Leo Stein died on 29 July 1947, just days after the appearance of *Appreciation*. But he did live long enough to see the first congratulatory reviews, which praised *Appreciation* as a superb introduction to modern art and an illuminating memoir. "Every artistic enterprise, whether by the artist or the audience, is a gamble," wrote Stein. This time, he had won.

NOTES

1. Alfred H. Barr Jr., *Matisse, His Art and His Public* (New York: Museum of Modern Art, 1951), 57.

2. Leo Stein to Mabel Weeks, [1905], quoted in Leo Stein, *Journey into the Self*, 15.

3. "I feel impelled to come over and see it." Emma Lootz Erving to Gertrude Stein, 13 December 1904, Yale Collection of American Literature.

4. "The New Return to Nature," *The New Republic,* 18 March 1916, 180.

5. "A New Salon in Paris," *The New Republic,* 30 July 1924, 272.

6. Leo Stein to Lee Simonson, 11 October 1913, Yale Collection of American Literature.

7. Ibid.

8. Jerome Mellquist, *New York Times Book Review*, 3 August 1947, 3.

9. "Art and the Frame," *The New Republic,* 24 March 1926, 143.

Foreword

A PHRASE of A. N. Whitehead's serves me well for an opening. "Life," he says, "is an offensive against the repetitive mechanisms of nature." Though the most recent science has weakened a little the nineteenth century's belief in mechanism, this change does not affect the practical world in which we live. Bricks may rise in the air if the free-moving electrons move just right, instead of staying on the ground as they commonly do, yet the probability that this will happen is measured by a figure one followed by noughts extending through thousands of miles. It may be to some a religious or philosophical comfort to know that this is possible, that nature cannot be proved a perfect mechanism and may dance an unexpected rigadoon. None the less, we cannot live as though fire would chill our cocktails and ice would cook our porridge. It is still practicable to oppose the apparently capricious life to the apparently mechanistic nature.

Life will have its way if it can, and resists submission to control. When it reaches the stage of foresight, this refusal to submit sets goals and devises means to reach them. All living things, even plants seeking sun and water, move toward the satisfaction of needs, but in man this becomes all-important and explicit. The offensive against the repetitive mechanisms of nature becomes a war with strategy and tactics.

Life at the human level has for this offensive numerous methods which I shall sketchily order in the second chapter of this book. Of these methods art is the particular one of which I propose to write here. I shall not do this systematically; I shall say as simply as I can things that I have found it useful to know, thinking that others too will find them useful. This is not a philosophy of art—for I agree with Santayana that such philosophy is verbiage, an attempt to systematize imponderables. Nor is it science, which in these matters cannot do much. It is a little debauch in the realm of ideas, the realm in which I delight to play and in which "I loaf and invite my soul, I lean and loaf at ease, observing a spear of summer grass." The greensward is the world of art, and incidentally of other things; for art is expression, and not remote from what it expresses. Art is, to use the English vulgarism, a bit of all right, but it is intimately connected with everything else—even with things that are all wrong, like murder and sudden death. Therefore anything and everything will incidentally come up and get such treatment as I can give it.

Art has often been concerned with religion, and something often said of religion can also be said of art: that it is what man does with his loneliness. The universe is so big and communication with one's fellowmen is so limited that men want both to understand and to be understood better than they can understand or be understood by their fellows. Religion is one way of getting these desires satisfied, and art is another. The real creation in these fields is solitary. The community is the matrix in which the individual grows, but it is the individual crystal that has form and is the occasion of more form. It is the individual who creates, and it is the individual who re-creates. Man, the social animal, likes to take his pleasures in company, but something must even then be done by the individual as such—unless each palate has its fineness of sense, the choicest wines are wasted, no matter how great the jollity. A man who collects in the spirit of a collector collects specimens, but for genuineness of personal experience specimens are of no importance. One might as well collect specimens of religion. For the student of comparative religion such a collection is useful, but for the religious person only that is useful which communicates or expresses religious values.

So it is for art. I am not a collector. In this book I am concerned with the kind of interest that is vital, which has centrally to do with the offensive against the mechanisms of nature. The choice of subjects and the manner of treatment are the results of this direction of interest.

Art is often taken to have some special relation to truth for which Keats is incessantly quoted: Beauty is truth,

truth, beauty. But Keats was here talking philosophy, and if one, using these words as they are commonly used, is accurate, art has nothing to do with truth essentially. Nor has beauty. Truth is not reality, but is what we say about reality. Art, however, is not what we say *about* anything. It is what we say. A portrait which is a work of art says something about its subject, but it might remain a work of art even if someone took it as a still life or a fanfare in blue and scarlet. Art is creation essentially. Science is also creation, but a scientific theory would be a useless creation if it did not tell a truth about the reality to which it refers. The artist, in so far as he is concerned with truth, is satisfied with the feeling of it, which is the same as the sense of reality, and so enjoys an independence which the scientist cannot share.

A creation in art stands on its own bottom. It is a kind of reality, and therefore lies to the farther side of truth. Its standards are not standards of truth but of reality. A real thing is one that withstands disintegration. So ice will melt when it encounters the temperature necessary to disintegrate it and ceases to be ice, and the reflection in a mirror that seems solid enough will disintegrate if the mirror becomes clouded. A work of art is a composition, and its persistent reality as a work of art depends on relations between the elements of this composition. "Right" relations make the composition real, and when the relations are not "right" the composition lacks reality and disintegrates. In that case, whatever other merits the work may have (melted ice may still serve as water) as a work of art it is a failure.

Art is the union of man and nature; its realities are essentially man-made. Science is the separation of man and nature, so far as in a man's universe this is possible. Science tries to see things as a disembodied intelligence, a robot intelligence, would see them. It prefers the testimony of a registering apparatus and pointer readings to the testimony of "a simple separate person." But without that simple separate person, there is no art. It is an advantage, to continue with Walt Whitman, "if one can utter the word Democratic, the word En-Masse," and speak not only for oneself, as some moderns do, but also for the many, as Homer and Shakespeare, Raphael and Rembrandt did. But the nub of art is the creation of something essentially human in terms of such relations as resist disintegration. When such a product has its own recognized vitality, it is successful art.

Art is the recurrent theme of this book, which makes of this individual creative experience its fundamental assumption. It looks on life as a going concern, and on art as one of the means to keep it going. It is entirely indifferent to conventions, rituals, orthodoxies, and it fairly foams at the mouth over the pretensions of the current orthodoxies. These foolish currencies which often think themselves to be the issues coming from the mint built on the topmost pinnacles of time, are really only moments in the variable river of events, are eddies having a duration truly, but a duration only as long as they spin: a little change in the river and they are swept away. Both life and art are too various to authenticate orthodoxies. These are refuges to cling to for those who fear the turbulencies of the stream; but for others they are merely definitions, precisions of some of the ways in which things can be taken. In this they are worthy of regard, even for those who cannot accept them.

The world since the Renaissance, and for all I know even before that, has been art conscious more than I think is good for it. Art is a sort of edge or point given to appreciation, and is really important when it is the edge or point to someone's genuinely felt appreciation. Appreciation is the kind of experience which comes to a consummation in art, and I now believe that by keeping art related to appreciation, one finds the best approach to this subject. Art as a fetish is absurd. Everybody who pretends to culture is supposedly obliged to an interest in things which are often of no real interest to him. This means ritual, not reality. It is quite false, and in this book I treat art sanely as a part of normal experience. Appreciation belongs to everybody, and for almost all, if not for all, it has its emergencies in art. Unless one thinks of art narrowly, no one is a stranger to it, though many have never sought for it the honor of an initial big letter.

Art is always with us, though Herbert Read can say (in *Art Now*) that never since the Baroque period has art served any social or cultural purpose. This statement I think absurd. It is true that religious art since then has been in eclipse, but there are other interests in society besides religion. French eighteenth century art was integrally part of French, even of European, culture, and the portrait painters of England italicize its eighteenth century. Landscape in the nineteenth century was vitally a worship. Its pantheism came to expression not only in poetry but in pictures, which were as important to its devotees as the pictures in the churches of Italy or Spain. The really holy pictures and statues, it must be remembered, were almost never, if ever, reputable works of art, whereas the sacred pictures of the nature lovers were. Nor is all art made with paint. Since photographic reproduction has become possible, drawings of immense social significance are appearing everywhere and all the time. The occasional Daumier, Gavarni, Rowlandson, have had innumerable followers. Any review of the month's news must include cartoons as well as print, and these cartoons are art, art, art. There is art from day to day, as well as art from century to century. One recalls a rare meal at the Tour d'Argent or Voisin's, but one eats bread day in day out. And bread also is food.

Art is no place for snobs. It is important because something has happened, and not because there is solemn or even reverent discourse about it. The museum is a necessary misfortune, and picture shows a worse one. It will be a happy moment when reproductions of paintings can be so perfectly made that originals can be left like first editions and manuscripts to makers of collections, while anyone can have a copy of his own which, like the printed book, is just as good. People then will have private galleries as they have their bookshelves, and there can be circulating galleries, and it will then be possible to get away from the absurdity of regarding it as important to visit shows and supposedly *see* in a few minutes scores of pictures that one will never meet again. This is no more than a bit of Vanity Fair with the same importance—neither more nor less—as visits to the other booths.

One has of late heard a lot about the Great Books. G. B. Stern, in her pleasant story *Thunderstorm,* tells how an Italian peasant enjoyed one of the greatest of these books.

She thoroughly enjoyed *Hamlet* as the blood and thunder story that it is. But too often the great books are read as Tennyson's Northern Farmer listened to the preacher, "An I thowt a said whot a owt to a said an' I comed awaäy." An artist puts into his work as much as he can of what he intends. The reader takes out of it as much as he can carry off. There may be or there may not be a close correlation between these two operations. Certainly there can be no standard of extraction, which, like stuff in cans guaranteed to be of a certain quality and strength, can be taken by everyone with confidence in the result. Every artistic enterprise, whether by the artist or the audience, is a gamble, and nothing can make it otherwise.

I wish to thank The Macmillan Company for permission to quote from Alfred North Whitehead's *Adventures in Ideas;* Doubleday and Company for quotations from Margaret Kennedy's *Red Sky at Morning;* and Harcourt, Brace and Company for quotations from Herbert Read's *Art Now.*

Contents

Introduction

THE MAN who can knock out Joe Louis is hard to find, but there are plenty of fighting men of one kind or another. The exceptional person is of course exceptional, but only because he is an unusual specimen of a kind that is common. Otherwise he is a freak. One can make an efficient army because there are many men who can carry a gun, who can read a map and make calculations, who can be trained or educated to fill all the roles from G I Joe to Eisenhower. So it is with art, which we have in all the forms from pulp magazines to that poem of Paul Valéry which took four years to write, though only four hundred lines long, and which no man can understand fully. James

Joyce told someone that he expected his earnest readers to spend their lives reading him. What he thought they would get out of it I do not know. Valéry is less sacramental. He says in effect, I wrote this to please myself; if someone else can get something out of it he is welcome, but I do not urge anyone to try.

The art of Valéry and Joyce is a rare kind, which calls for intense devotion and persistent effort both from author and reader, but there is also art which is so simple and everyday that the artist who creates it is not even aware that he is one. Somebody who has never thought of such a thing may be walking along a country road and may see trees and houses, fields and hills, streams, clouds, sky. Nothing there cries aloud to him, "I am a landscape"; yet a landscape may appear before his eyes. The landscape didn't make itself, he made it, and anyone who makes anything like this is an artist. The desire may grow on him to be a painter also. He may say to himself, "Gee, I'd like to paint that." And if he gets some paint and brushes, some advice, and has the necessary patience, he will be a painter—like Winston Churchill. I have never seen a picture by Churchill. All I know about him as an artist is that some years ago, when he was in Florence, he wanted to know about Cézanne. Charles Loeser, who had Cézannes, showed them and tried to explain, but Churchill, he told me, was not much enlightened. Nor was he discouraged—for he still paints when there is time and occasion.

Art is not necessarily a serious matter and I want to avoid all pretentiousness in treating of it. Art and genius are both common everyday things, and are not essentially different in their little and their great occasions. It is true that they seem different, but that is a result of conventional ways of thinking. The elder moralists and poets of old were continually reminding people that kings were only mortals like the rest of mankind. I want to insist that making up a package of candy at Maillard's is art not altogether different from a picture by Renoir. Santayana, in *The Last Puritan,* tells how Rose received gifts from Mario attractively done up. Before she undid them she paused with pleasurable feeling at the art shown in the wrapping. She didn't say to herself, "This is art," nor do I when I look at a favorite picture by Domenico Veneziano. But we both recognize a quality which is called artistic, and what is artistic is art. A dainty package is a simple form of the same kind of art as that of Mondrian, just as a well-proportioned box is a simple bit of architecture. A grocer doing up a pound of cheese has nothing of that sort on his mind. Every action having as its purpose to give satisfaction to one's interest in forms is art. Art is not a king by divine right. Art is a democracy where all are equal before the law of choice; all are called, though few are chosen for the museum shrine.

What is true of art is true of genius. Of few things is there so much pretentious nonsense current. William James said that genius was the capacity to get into a biographical dictionary, but I think even this an understatement. Genius is simply creativity, and its opposite is routine. Both creativeness and routine are common. The academic artist is at bottom a man of routine, however much he may play at variation. The creative artist is a revolutionary, even though the revolution is gradually and almost imperceptibly effected.

Of course genius is mysterious, but so is routine. Professor Levy, a distinguished English physicist, says that no one can explain why, when we pull a piece of paper by one corner, the rest of it comes along. Though the man in the street does not think this mysterious, it is as mysterious as anything whatever. The mysterious is neither more nor less than that for which we have no technique of investigation. When we successfully investigate something, it ceases to be mysterious. Life is a mystery because it cannot be reduced to anything else. The atom was a mystery until it was broken up. The great is rarer than the little, but not a whit more mysterious. Shakespeare's creative powers were enormous and mine are slight, but if I were not something of a genius—that is, if I had no creative powers—I couldn't write this book, which is certainly not a matter of mere routine. So too, I have muscles in my arm that are not essentially different from those of Joe Louis. His have more punch in them, that is all.

It is, I believe, a good thing to recognize the continuity of the usual and the unusual, and if we are to be reverent it is better to be widely and not narrowly reverent. It is better to recognize creativity as something common and to cultivate it generally, than to suppose that those who have it more are different in kind. I believe that this regard for genius in its littleness is on the whole more important than regard for its bigness. That will take care of itself, but the little of it is likely to be obscured.

We hear much of the need to teach people to use language properly. There is no difficulty in teaching them the routine of expression (yours of the fifteenth ult. received and contents noted), but it is good to make them realize that there is no essential difference between them and those who write, except interest, use and purpose—that creativity in writing means nothing more than fitting words accurately and specifically to what one specifically and accurately intends. Shakespeare certainly intended more than most and had exceptional gifts, but anyone who has anything to say and wants to interest the receiver has a like object. Every personal letter one writes, every personal statement one makes, may be creative writing if one's interest is to make it such. Most people do not have this interest; what they write in ordinary communications is as dull as they can make it. They have never been taught to think of all writing as in its degree *writing* and all speaking *speaking,* and so they write in rubber stamps and speak in the current routine or slang, as though writing and speaking was something reserved for the elect. We can understand Shakespeare if we know his language and are sufficiently interested really to read him—that is, to read him with attention—and we can understand Einstein on the same terms. This is true because, although we cannot create the great things they have done, we can re-create them, and we can do this because we have some measure of creative power, which they stimulate. To make the most of this is the vital purpose of education.

What there is of system in this little book has as its directive the notion that continuity illuminates. Art that is definitely taken as art is no more than the remarking, the sharpening and the fixing of experiences that may be noted in the affairs of every day, and the value of the great things is made more valuable when they are known as exceptional, not in their kind but in their degree. There must be classifications if general statements are to be made, and it is a good thing if one can find classifications that are simple and fresh.

Conventional thinking uses conventional classifications that are taken to be natural and inevitable, although in great part they lead to confusion. People speak as though they mean one thing when they really intend something else. A typical instance is that of the British Constitution, which even such clever politicians as the Founding Fathers did not really understand because the words used to describe it were fictitious. Not till Bagehot, well on in the nineteenth century, described it in terms which actually fitted it, did people stop thinking and speaking of it in terms that did not fit. It is a misfortune of our present culture that so much of our creative energy goes into our enormously available propaganda and so little into the precising of meanings, which is for the most part left to the men of science. Veracity means not lying, and nothing more stands in the way of veracity than words like *democracy, liberty, good will, liberal culture, ideals* and hundreds of other words, which sound as though they mean something particular but really mean anything or nothing. Instead of talking with detailed precision, which would show one's hand, or more precisely, one's mind and morals, one uses these inspirational, but to the critical mind, depressing words. There is no flattering unction laid to the soul more damning than holy words that cover realities with which holiness has nothing to do, and the first need of a substantial education is to learn the relation of words to things.

It has often been said that the particular distinction of

Shakespeare's style is that the words are the things to which they apply. This is the greatest quality that writing can have, and it can be learned to the degree that for anyone it is possible only by an acquired practice of knowing what one wants to say, and then saying it without in the meantime losing contact with one's subject matter. Logic will not help if one forgets the precise thing that one wants to say.

The same holds true for reading. It is astonishing how often someone will tell you what he has read in a book or in the papers, and when you read it you find nothing of the kind. If you ask to have it pointed out, it isn't there. Good writing and reading are really a simple matter, though not an easy one. Everybody knows that a machine will not work well if the parts are not properly fitted and adjusted. It is exactly the same with the mind. Words are the tools and if they are not fitted to the work and accurately applied, they are not only bad in themselves but fruitful of mischief. It makes much less difference what you read than how you read it. Whatever one reads with close attention to the words and also to the things the words mean is the instrument of a liberal culture; whatever one reads otherwise, whether philosophy or history or poetry, is not. The habit of veracity, of not pretending, is fundamental. To understand one must know the dictionary meaning of words, but one cannot stop at that. I was once asked to correct the translation of a book from the German that had been made by a person meticulously careful to look up in the dictionary all words not familiar. There must have been many of these words, for though every word used had a dictionary warrant, the sentences were almost meaningless. One should think in things with the aid of words. Word thinking is robot thinking. "Aristotelian logic . . . is the fertile matrix of fallacies," says Whitehead. Like a calculating machine it assures that the result shall be correct, but not that it shall make sense. The things to which the words refer are the normal checks on the mere mechanics of thinking, and when these are neglected we become the easy victims of propaganda.

There are men so rich in words that they can spend them unceasingly and still always have more, like filibustering senators. I once met a perfect specimen of this sort. He talked and talked and said nothing. Suddenly he stopped and looked distressed.

"I look pretty healthy, don't I?" he said.

I assured him that he did.

"You wouldn't suppose I was suffering from an incurable disease, would you?"

"Certainly not."

"Well, I am: incurable, utterly incurable, utterly incurable."

"But what can it possibly be?"

"Diarrhea of words, constipation of ideas," he exploded.

He was the adjuster for a railroad company and well fitted to the job of talking accident cases into taking the least possible compensation. In the sixty years since this meeting I have often had reason to think of him and tell his sad story, for though he was a rare specimen of his kind, the kind is not at all rare.

Pleasure in clear hard thinking is not so common as it ought to be in a democracy that has before it so many difficult problems as ours. "All propositions for the reorganization of society must have their complexities, which may need half an hour of explanation, and half an hour of explanation is nine and twenty minutes too much for the average man," says H. G. Wells somewhere. Only highbrows are so extravagant of intellectual effort. If the average man reads about these things, he wants the solution without being bothered to understand the problem. This saves thinking, and what he reads is in any case usually so encumbered with tendentious language as to be most innutritious food for thought. Even a real thinker would find his thinking machine gummed by the flood of sticky words. The average man does not of necessity object to clear language, provided it expresses his prejudices, and therefore certain very good writers are also popular writers. The readers of the papers for which they write are prepared to take them for granted, and do so. It pleases them to be of the same mind as eminent authorities, and it would surprise them much to learn that the eminent authorities do not understand these writings as the enthusiastic reader does. Often I have tried to make clear to someone who entirely agreed with me that he didn't agree with me at all—but generally in vain. Usually he begins to have a headache before the stage is reached where such fine discriminations become clear.

Nor does the average man think such distinctions important. This reminds me of two admirable Britons that Mahonri Young once told me about. The National Gallery had bought a Titian for a great price, and Young saw these gentlemen approach the picture from opposite sides, each reading a paper. They met before it and identified it. Then one said, "I don't see the value in it." The other said,

"Neither do I," and both shook their heads in skeptical resignation and departed, to meditate on the foolish extravagance of the government. So it is generally when one tries to make the average man see the importance of exact thinking. He regards it as an extravagant demand. He can understand exactness in a machine, but the same quality in a mind is beyond the limits of his interest.

The subject of this book is Prose and Poetry, and it may seem that all this has little to do with a theme that smells of esthetics. But as I see it, this kind of thing is the very heart of the subject. I dislike estheticism. For me Prose and Poetry belong to the world of vital interests, to those matters which affect the current of our days. They are less important than food and shelter, but as soon as we can sit back and reflect, they become important enough to be worth bothering about, even to the point of having a book written about them.

I

What the Book Is About

A COMPREHENSIVE anthology of English Poetry like the four volume Ward's *English Poets* has within its ample limits writing of many kinds. It all passes as poetry, and we may fairly say that it is all poetry. But usually when poetry is defined the definitions are so limited that they cut out much, or even most, of what so passes as poetry. A proper definition should include everything that belongs, and exclude everything that does not. A definition of poetry must therefore be wide in its scope. As I believe that no such definition is possible, I shall not try to make one, but instead I shall try to give an intelligible meaning to the adjective "poetic."

That seems to me both practicable and useful. Throughout this book I shall be concerned with a fundamental distinction, that between the poetic and the prosaic. By the poetic or poetical (for it is not worth while trying to keep a difference between these two forms), I shall mean that which communicates appreciations; and by the prosaic that which makes statements, that which analyzes, that which is factual in character, that which is concerned with use. There are things that in the ordinary sense of the word we use, and others that we do not. When a man says to his wife, "That wall is too bare; I'll get a picture for it," it is obvious that the picture is to be used. He wants a modified arrangement of the room for which the picture is to serve. That is using it. But when one looks at the picture which one has hung in place, one is not in any ordinary sense of the word using it. The picture has changed from an object of use to one of appreciation.

This word appreciation has, I believe, been too much neglected, though there is no other that I can think of that will take its place. Appreciation names all the ways in which we regard things that we do not define, measure or directly use. For instance, a man choosing an employee for some particular purpose considers qualities that he cannot test. He has to size up the man—which is an act of appreciation, different from dictating a letter to see how accurate his stenography is. A detective studying a man's character does a similar thing, and so may a man to whom another is introduced, or a painter beginning on a portrait. The portrait which results from the painter's appreciation is what we call art. The actions of the others do not have any such end, but I wish to keep art closely related to other things. Art should be taken importantly only when there is a good reason.

I remember that years ago when Mrs. Mackay was not satisfied with a portrait that Meissonier had painted, she paid the large price demanded, and then burned the picture. Her action seemed to many almost as pernicious as though she had burned the painter at the stake. Milton said that one had as good murder a man as murder a good book, but I doubt whether he would have thought that a portrait of Mrs. Mackay could be put in the same class with good books.

In a French comedy one man says to another, "But Monsieur Durand, don't you believe that art should be protected?"

"Art of course, but not the artists, who are a lot of ne'er-do-wells and rascals."

For Monsieur Durand art was holy, just as the flag is holy for people who care little for the land or the people. With this attitude toward art we never can get to the bottom of it, and I like to get to the bottom of things. So we are here going to have art treated as just one of the ways in which appreciations are recorded. The businessman just mentioned records his appreciation by employing the man or rejecting him, the detective perhaps by writing a report, the painter by posing the model in a certain way and adopting a certain treatment in the portrait. The differences in the way of recording the appreciations result in the three classes of things: the instrumental, the informational or prosaic, and the poetical. The businessman puts his employee to work, which is using him instrumentally; the detective writes a report, which is to give information and also to tell what his appreciation was; the painter does a portrait which communicates his appreciation. Anyone who looks at the portrait understandingly will share immediately the painter's experience, while in the other cases there is nothing of this immediacy. The three ways of putting things on record which are also related to the interests that determine the appreciations, I shall call in a rough way practice, science and art—one concerned with using, one with knowing, one with renewing appreciation. The distinctions are, of course, not clean-cut—few distinctions are —but they are sufficiently clear to be useful, and that is all that I ask of them.

The practical, the prosaic and the poetic are inextricably mixed up in the actual process of living. One may at the same time use a motor to go somewhere, be keenly observant of how it works, and enjoy its smooth-running adaptation to its purpose. There is writing that is predominantly prosaic, and writing that is predominantly poetic, like scientific formulae and lyric poems, but there is much writing which is not one or the other in so obviously simple a way—the *Sermon on the Mount, Isaiah,* most oratory, preaching, fiction.

Nor is this distinction limited to expression in words. A drawing may be a diagram to be blueprinted; it may be a fantasy by Botticelli or Paul Klee; it may be a cartoon by Daumier or Mauldin; it may be an advertisement for cars or perfumes. The diagram is undoubtedly prose, the Botticelli and the Paul Klee undoubtedly poetry, but all the rest are more or less of both. The diagram enlightens and is utilized, the fantasies are only for appreciation, but the others are to be used for information or satire, to tell about certain conditions existing somewhere and also to be appreciated.

Appreciation is often withheld from things because they aren't labeled as the proper objects thereof. For instance, a man named Hambidge made interesting discoveries in proportions used by the Greeks in all their arts, and many Greek vases in American museums were measured and found to conform to the formulae that Hambidge had worked out. Then someone discovered the same proportions in pots and pans, and this has been cited as discrediting Hambidge. I can't see why. If the Greeks had formulae by which ordinary utensils could be given good proportions, so much the better; this may happen by chance or through the contriver's taste, even in pots and pans. The average man finds poetry only where it is labeled, but the artist will frequently find it elsewhere and bring it to the notice of all the world.

The word "poetic" is often used to mean "fanciful" or "dreamy," just as "prosaic" is used to mean "dull" or "pedestrian"; but good poetry is not fanciful or dreamy for the most part. It is substantial, just as good prose is far other than dull or pedestrian. Good words like these have possibilities of use beyond such degradation, and should be salvaged. It is best to get rid of all derogatory words in art, and all flattering ones. I believe that one cannot do better than with "poetic" and "prosaic" for general use. Common wine and whiskey bottles are not usually beautiful, as Italian wine flasks so often are, but slight changes in their proportions can make them so, and introduce into the container something of the poetic value which already exists for the contained. Makers of perfumes try to make their bottles poetic as well as their labels; sometimes they are admirably successful, more successful with the bottles than with the labels, perhaps. I think that much is gained by letting "poetic" become a common term, rather than a snobbish one. Some may object that in this way the word is vulgarized. A word cannot be vulgarized except by being misapplied.

"Almost all absurdity of conduct arises from imitation of those whom we cannot resemble," said Dr. Johnson. What is vulgarity in conduct is also vulgarity in language. Nothing is vulgar because it is common. There is poetic expression which is better or worse, wise or silly; there is that which is firsthand, and that which is vulgarized or made absurd by imitation of that which it cannot resemble. Let it be called bad poetry, but to say that poetry which is bad is not poetry is to talk nonsense. One says yes and another says no; one says a house is not a house unless it is full of gadgets, and another says it is a house if it has a roof and something to hold that up. Best call both houses, and make distinctions within the class.

There is profit by being hard-headed in these matters, and ultimately veracity will be the gainer. Let it be clearly understood then that "prosaic" is to mean what is for knowledge and utility, and that "poetic" has to do with appreciation; that most things in this world lend themselves to use, knowledge and appreciation; that as dirt is matter in the wrong place, so vulgarity is appreciation in the wrong place. There can be as much vulgarity in the appreciation of Cézanne or Van Gogh as in the appreciation of a perfume; there can be as much recorded in a painting hung in a museum as in an advertisement for hosiery. The world today is much worried about education, so here is an opening that I consider of much importance. One can train by routine, but one can educate only by awakening consciousness of things. There is no better awakener of consciousness than classification that cuts across routine, and simple classifications are best, such as I here propose. I believe that the sequel will show that the scheme is really useful.

All vital appreciation has a certain simplicity, though the simplification is not always immediate. Very few people can appreciate the poetry of Paul Valéry. When a man spends four years writing four hundred lines, it is probable that one would have to spend a lot of time reading them. But if one can never reach the stage of simple appreciation of this poetry one has never reached the stage of complete appreciation. Even if understood in an explanatory way—that is, prosaically—the poetic appreciation remains imperfect. Matisse spent three years and more than a hundred sittings on a small statue, which at the end looked to the average person as though it might have been done in an afternoon. One might explain to someone that this was not a sketch, as it appeared to be, but a peculiarly penetrating study; and the person, if docile, might understand what you were trying to tell him, but if at the end he didn't see it as it would appear if he had made the discovery for himself, his appreciation is not complete. I had seen this figure in plaster several times and admired it, but it was only when I saw it in bronze that my enthusiasm flamed, and I bought it.

When one fully realizes a successful work of art one finds it to be a kind of just-so story. There is a place for everything, and everything is in its place. The layman cannot understand why the artist keeps on fiddling with his picture when to all appearances it is done, even overdone. Some one who visited Titian tells that he had a lot of pictures standing against the wall of his studio, and that he would examine them with a hostile eye, as though they were his worst enemies. Degas was proverbial for this everlasting dissatisfaction with his paintings—the feeling that after all, even when most finished, they were still not just-so. Henri Rouart, the great French collector, had a picture considered the best of his many pictures by Degas, that Degas was always wanting to retouch. The story was that Rouart held it to the wall with a padlock. I asked M. Rouart about this, and he said the padlock was a fiction but that he kept his eye on Degas when Degas left the house after his customary dinner on Thursday, even though the picture was a little large to be hidden under the painter's cape. It is not everyone who can see well enough to comprehend the artist's dissatisfaction with his work, but the nearer he comes to this, the better he understands the work. Entire possession is the rarely fulfilled goal of the creative process. Masterpieces are not many.

This chapter, which is intended to tell what this book is about, has been a rambling one. Other chapters will develop the various themes a little more systematically, but not very. I don't think this a subject for much system. I once wrote a systematic book on esthetics in which all my fondness for logical development was given the loose, and I haven't found that most readers like that. When I read it lately, I didn't like it very much myself. This book will not err on that side, though it may on the other.

II

The Two Crosses

THE POETIC and the prosaic have their place in a rich complex of activities, and the purpose of this chapter is so to place them. The most complicated of all forms of living is what we call practice, and it is also the most familiar. In consequence one does not commonly recognize that it is the least simple. But in fact a little of everything goes into it, and simplification comes when we specialize. For usefulness of illustration, therefore, I begin with a manufacturer. At the other end of the scale is a state of being which is not far removed from nullity. It is a condition familiar to many who on occasion have looked out fixedly and vacantly for so long as almost to lose consciousness, and return to life with a start. Between these extremes lies the series of states that has to do specifically with knowing and appreciating, that is, with science and art. To arrange all this in a scheme may be helpful.

The everyday life in business and society is a complicated affair to which no kind of mental activity is lacking. A manufacturer of textiles has to adjust his finances and overlook his machines. He must use intuition in choosing his employees and picking designs for the cloths to be woven. There are actions which are purely intellectual, and others in which feeling predominates. He may like a design, but know that it would be too expensive to produce. What he would prefer may be something that he thinks the public would reject. There is a crisscross of all things in his mind in the daily round of complicated employments.

Such a man we call a practical man. Less "practical" men specialize. The practical man is at one moment essentially the man of science, not perhaps looking for brand new solutions for hitherto unknown problems, but dealing with situations that are particular and more or less novel, that are technical situations of finance or mechanics, and that must be treated analytically, which is the method of science. At another moment he is the artist, dealing with values, appreciating and working with them. The scientist and the artist develop further these specialties, though they do not cease entirely to be "practical," for they still deal with an existent material.

The scientist is a man who applies pure thought, that is, logic, and if possible, mathematics, to the heterogeneous facts of nature. He is not a pure thinker, for he lives in a mixed world. For him there remains always the world of things which have appreciable qualities. When the agricultural college at Berkeley was being projected, a dirt farmer who offered his advice did not see the need for such a school. He said, "When I want to know about a soil I smell it, and taste it, and roll it between my fingers, and then I know all about it." Professor Hilgard, who was to be the director of the "Cow College," assured him that the pupils would be taught to do all this, and to analyze the soil as well. There are sciences, like physics, where this kind of thing counts for little; and others, like medicine, where it still counts for a great deal.

For the artist there is something analogous. His pure contemplation of values, his pure appreciation, is disturbed by the multiplicity of the world before him. People often think of the poet as simply having something organically growing in his soul. There is that beautiful word "inspiration." They do not realize the heterogeneity of his material, and the large amount of critical discrimination needed to put it in order. When we look at a landscape, with its harmony of mood, the blending of all the elements that compose it, we do not stop to think that those elements have for the most part nothing to do with each other, that they belong together only in the vision of the artist, and that to a closer observer the heterogeneity is overwhelming.

Many, many years ago, it occurred to me to notice that the elements of the human face were really ugly in the disparity of their textures, and that one advantage of art in representing them was the unity of the material. I was quite obsessed by this for a while and was continually noticing it. Once I was in the Duomo in Sienna with a young lady who was curious and liked to hear things discussed. I was talking of this and said, "If you notice the way your eyebrows are stuck into the skin, the ugly contrast of hair and forehead, the glassy surface of the eyes, the edges of the skin and lip-membrane," and so on and so on. The young lady in question was an international beauty, known in all the capitals of Europe, with whom the Crown Prince of Germany, then a very nice young boy, had just fallen violently in love; who was used to being admired, praised, courted, and who afterwards married a duke. She listened gravely to my demonstration, even admired my single-mindedness, and then turned smilingly to a friend with us and said, "Did you ever in your life hear a man talk like that before?" The moment for the demonstration was not well chosen, but it is true that the more closely things are looked at, the more heterogeneous they appear.

For music the heterogeneity of the elements is less than for the other arts. These elements are tones, and not, as for literature, noises made communicable. Words, because they are only noises, will not stand close examination. I do not know how common it is for children to do as I used to do when I was quite little—repeat a word rapidly over and over again until it became a mere sound, and I wondered how it could ever have come to mean cat or dog or horse. One cannot completely dissociate meanings and sounds. A Japanese said that the most beautiful word in English was "cellardoor." This had not occurred to me, and never would have, but as soon as I heard this I remembered that "celadon," which is so much like it, had always seemed to me a word of unusual beauty. Shelley and shelly do not sound alike, nor do Abraham the

Prophet and Abraham Lincoln. It is even difficult for me to believe that "Cromwell, fling away ambition" is the same name as the Cromwell that goes with Oliver. Art deals with matters that do not exist in a vacuum which permits them to have sharp and unmistakable contours; nor does it, except to some extent for music, deal with a stuff that, like refined chemicals, is pure. Art deals with matters that are quite otherwise, ones which are not only heterogeneous but for which intuition, appreciation, is obstructed—ones in which it is possible by a somewhat misdirected attention to break up the unity of the whole, to become analytic and destructive.

Music as the purest of the arts suffers least from this, and is the natural way of transition from art to mysticism. The work of art, if successful, is always a whole. If you take away from art its stuff, its material substance, and in consequence its form, then what you have left is the immaterial substance of the mystic experience. For many mysticism means quite definitely religion, and no doubt it has a religious flavor, but it need have no more than this. Essentially it is the feeling of an ineffable whole, in which nothing can be precisely expressed because nothing can be precisely laid hold of. Its analogue on the side of the intellect is logic, which today is seen to be the same as pure mathematics, where everything comes nearest to being laid hold of in its detailed essentiality. Mysticism is the purest intuition, and pure mathematics is the purest thinking. It is so purely thinking that some latter-day philosophers who came to philosophy from mathematical physics think that God may be the Absolute Mathematician.

The philosopher's God is perhaps necessarily what he would be if he were God. The God of the intuitive, appreciative mind is as different as possible from this. The intellect is analytic and makes for differences, the appreciative mind wants rather to wash out differences. It accepts differences only as these are needed to make up a varied whole. It is interested in what is alike, and is constantly looking for and spontaneously finding analogies. The scientific mind finds that things which are apparently simple are really complicated, and it proceeds to break them up. It finds wholes to be different and only elements to be alike, at times even identical. The appreciative mind neglects elements and finds wholes to be similar. Mathematics is the absolute complexity stated in general terms, and mysticism is the felt absolute simplicity for which there are no terms. The whole of mathematics fills many volumes; the expression of a perfect mysticism will not admit of so much as a word.

"If what Jacob has to say is ineffable, Jacob [Boehme] should not try to say it." Thus the downright Dr. Johnson. All expression of mysticism and also mystical poetry fails to be pure enough symbol; the factual matter of the symbol is commonly too intrusive. I know only one mystical poem that is satisfactorily successful: *The Obscure Night of the Soul,* by St. John of the Cross. In that amazing poem, what is said counts for almost nothing, but is sublimated into the purposed significance. The artist does not intend to go so far as that, but in seeking an incorruptible unity, he is always something of a mystic. Unlike the mystic, he clings to the world of things, though he transmutes it. He can never say the whole of what he means, but the mystic cannot say at all what he means; for his meaning is something singular and indivisible, something absolute in its inexpressibility. The simple lover in Cyrano can only say "I love you," but the poet Cyrano can say the same thing in a hundred elaborated ways.

Music is transitional to mysticism, because it makes no particular statement, although its expression is so penetrating and so ample. The most purely poetic form of poetry, the lyric, is most like music. If you don't quite understand the meaning of, "What's oft been thought but ne'er so well expressed," you get little from this line of Pope. But I have noticed again and again in rereading familiar lyric poems that I had never noticed the exact meaning of this line or that. It is even probable that I had on occasion noticed it, but the enduring impression had been so little dependent on this meaning that it had faded, leaving only the music and the generalized meaning of the whole.

Science and art are clearly distinguished as knowing and appreciating, and even more absolutely are logic and mysticism as distinguishing and identifying, but there are certain human interests that confound them in certain ways. There are, in especial, philosophy and religion. Diagrammatically one might say that philosophy is a cross between art and logic, and religion a cross between mysticism and science. Religion would like at once to apprehend the world and to account for it, philosophy to rationalize and picture it. The religious want a mythology and salvation; only the theologian wants a metaphysic. "Science suggests a cosmology and whatever suggests a cosmology suggests a religion," says Whitehead. For philosophy, logic is too empty and art too disorderly, but a judicious mixture gives at least the appearance of an orderly world with plenty of stuff to make it interesting. If we examine it closely and it is not "our philosophy," it breaks down, the logic and the intuition do not meet in a perfect joint; but for as long as it holds, what I say applies. Of course these comments are only impressionistic. There are many kinds of religion and many kinds of philosophy, so many that they all arouse suspicion, and nothing can be summarily said about them that is more than an impression. But here is enough of exactitude for my present purposes.

When one has followed through the scheme of mental activity from science to logic and from art to mysticism one is fairly at an end. But one can perhaps speak of a state beyond, where mind is not entirely in abeyance, where there is something not yet death, but a kind of suspension of conscious life. This we can call Nirvana, and so offer something which lies at the opposite pole from the multifarious activity of the practical life. Some moments we all know when we come back with a jerk to the realization that we have been momentarily away from the world where things happen. So this limbo, if not a state that can endure, is one which is not unfamiliar.

This chapter serves to situate the poetic and the prosaic in the general scheme of things. In the practical life we are concerned with them without stopping to become aware of them. In art and science we know that we are dealing with them, and in mysticism and logic we are dealing with their abstracted values. Beyond, there is nothing except "absence of mind," and so we can stop here and next take up Poetry and Prose as our central theme.

III

Of Poetry and Prose

Coleridge spoke well and wisely about poetry and prose, distinguishing clearly between this pair and the other pair of prose and verse. Nothing of importance, so far as I know, has been said about them since. It is well known that poetry is not concerned with factual matters, and no one would today write a treatise on agriculture or on the science of the atom in the form of a poem. Something has of late been gleaned from psychoanalysis, and we have made acquaintance with the unconscious, but what we have learned from that does not bear particularly on this subject. Of course one comes on generalizations on this matter, as on all others, but they are for the most part the kind of generalizations made by literary amateurs and not by scientific students. The degree of accuracy possible when one deals with art does not amount to science in any rigorous sense. What is possible is rather intelligently discriminated description, of which there are good examples in the books of A. C. Barnes. In this book I am attempting nothing of that kind, for which I have no special talent. My interest is rather in ideas, ideas which seem to me significant and stimulating, but which do not amount either to science or philosophy. I believe in only one "ism" and that is a rather harmless one, at least as I take it. I am a pragmatist, by which I mean that the only sense I can give to the word "truth" is that it is a state of belief, and therefore a personal matter, and what cannot be taken in a context of other things can't be talked about. Therefore I take no interest in ultimate problems, and look for no final solutions. I am satisfied if we can get on in a promising direction. That is all that I want to do here.

No one has ever given a satisfactory definition of poetry as distinguished from prose, and I don't think that anyone ever will. It is like trying to distinguish definitely a working man and a man of leisure. For social purposes this is practicable, but if we try to be exact we find that every man does some work, and every man has some leisure. No exactness is possible in terms which are terms of more or less. There is in poetry more of the poetic than there is in prose and there is less of the prosaic, but neither the one nor the other is pure. Therefore I am not going to deal with prose and poetry at all, but with the prosaic and the poetic. By prosaic I mean having the quality of prose, and by poetic, of course, having the quality of poetry. I want to find the most intelligible meaning that I can for these terms.

A fact familiar to everyone, a word used by everybody, is for the present purpose brimful of instruction, and yet I have never seen its significance noted. If it hadn't taken me so long to hit upon this I should be surprised that it had not been long since a commonplace. It is obvious—that is to say, it lies right across our road—but it is not evident. That is, it does not, as the French say, jump to the eyes.

I refer to the familiar fact that we use the word *composition* in music as we do not use it for poetry and painting. We call musical works compositions and their authors composers, but we speak of composition *in* painting and poetry, and we call their makers painters and poets. It is true that painters like Whistler have taken suggestions from music and have called their works compositions, opus 1, 2, 3, and so on, and that much modern painting, and some writing, is explicitly composition, but no general conclusions have, so far as I know, been drawn. I think that such conclusions can be usefully drawn to make a broad classification.

That music is the purest of the arts needs no discussion because this is not questioned. Some believe it to be the greatest of the arts, but claims to importance are made on every side as they are made for every profession and way of life. But that music is the purest of the arts is undisputed. All the arts tend toward music. Architecture has been called frozen music. Tennyson told in a letter how sometimes he reached the limits of poetical expression and wanted to go over into music. Later I shall tell how it served me for completing incomplete landscape appreciations. If music is the purest of the arts, and if composition is its special character, some important conclusions should follow.

Children like composition. This is shown both in their drawings and in the gibberish in which they delight. When I was a small boy I heard my older high-school brother crooning, "The limit of the product of a constant and a variable is the product of the constant and the limit of the variable." I got to be as fond of it as I was of Captain Nemo's (*Twenty Thousand Leagues Under the Sea*), "If you will confound statics and dynamics, Professor, you will fall into serious error." I had no idea what either sentence meant, but I thought them both wonderful, and when I believed someone to be talking nonsense I would often say, "If you will confound statics and dynamics, Professor, you will fall into serious error."

In one class at school we had to learn by heart rules of grammar. Two I have never forgotten, and have always enjoyed: "A noun is the name of anything" and "A preposition is a word introducing a phrase modifier and showing the relation in sense between its principal word and the word modified." General Grant said that he learned in school that a noun is the name of a thing. Note the difference between these two definitions of a noun, one full-based and massive in its composition, and the other a mere statement with its loose-hanging end. I might have remembered the second definition, but I could never have enjoyed it. The definition of the preposition is also admirable, with its swing and swirl, its forward and backward movement. On a small scale it is like Wordsworth's yew trees—"With intertwisted fibres serpentine, upcoiling and inveterately convolved." What made all these sentences admirable was their form. Two I understood and two I didn't, but all four seemed important. In those that were understood, there was still something more important than was defined. In short, they had poetic value.

That prose and verse should in any way get mixed with prose and poetry, though today everyone knows that they are different, is unfortunate. How unrelated they are can be shown statistically by reference to good authorities. Henley published an excellent anthology of lyric poetry, and was so meticulous as to exclude even Gray's *Elegy in a Country Churchyard* as insufficiently lyrical, yet he put in forty selections from the Bible. Of these Logan Pearsall Smith, in his most discriminating *Treasury of English Prose,* includes eight, and Quiller-Couch in the *Oxford Book of English Prose* four. The same words can apparently be taken in different ways; that is, they can be read variously for various values.

My thesis is that there is no such thing as poetry or as prose—that these words, if they are to be used with intelligible accuracy, should be given an adjectival and not a nominal form; that in case this is done, the words become far more practicable and far less annoying. We need never ask of any work whether it is prose or poetry, whether it has demerits of category and ought to be otherwise because it is this or that kind of thing—for, outside music, which is the purest poetry, we can have no pure poetry except nonsense. What we ordinarily call nonsense is, however, not pure nonsense, but, as in Lear and Lewis Carroll, nonsensical; pure nonsense, except in refrains, is childish. There is in all art composition, and generally there is something else. This other thing I shall call construction.

Take architecture as convenient to demonstrate the difference. The engineer constructs, and the architect composes. Of course they don't have to be two different persons. A building that was not constructed would not stand; and if it was not composed, it would have no value as art. Very often the only consideration of the builder is to get as much usable space as possible, and so proportions and rhythm are entirely neglected. Many façades in Italy, compared with those in America, give an impression of massiveness out of all relation to their actual size, because the wall space, relative to the windows, is so much greater, and so much better proportioned. The lighting of the rooms is bad and space is wasted: there is failure of constructive utility, but composition is effective.

In music (of which I know next to nothing) scales, counterpoint, harmony, are, I suppose, constructive, and melody, fugue, sonata and other forms are composition.

Literature is the most varied and complex of the arts, for literature is words put to use, and words are the habitual instruments of communication. For constructive purposes words are used literally as in science: their purpose is simply to make sense. If one does not know what the words in a statement only intended for information mean, or if the words are not properly put together, one does not get their constructive value. For constructive purposes grammar and logic are important, even mandatory, but when composition is the main concern these can be scattered to the winds. Allusiveness and ellipsis fight it out with grammar and logic. "The heart has its reasons which the mind does not know," said Pascal. So it is with composition and construction.

For the graphic arts, compositional deformation has become a commonplace since Cézanne. The cubists pretended to something more, to deform not only composition but construction also, to analyze forms. But there was, in my opinion, only a pretense of rationality in their processes, only pseudo-rationality. This will be dealt with later. Construction in the graphic arts as well as in the others, is a matter of literalness; it is a means for telling what is presented, and not for what is implied. For composition, construction is only the underpinning, the armature, the factual basis, which composition generally recognizes and often scorns.

To some extent this distinction is like that of content and form, but it is by no means identical. It also, by being definitely connected with operations, with actions, avoids the mystic vagueness of these consecrated but hard-to-be-understood terms. As the demonstration goes forward, it will be seen how very different is the meaning of the words I use.

In science we avoid deformation. Things are taken as though no interests were involved except the general interest in finding out about things. If some particular is selected for especial attention, it is dissected out from the mass, but it does not deform the whole; one who is studying the nervous tract tries to keep it structurally related to the rest of the body. But a man who makes a composition is a particular person. His composition expresses his own interest, and this interest deforms the picture. In so doing, he passes out of the realm of prose into that of fiction, which is that of poetry.

Though composition is a particular thing, some general

statements can be made to help in ordering its complexities. One can't be rigorous in these things, which are capable of only vague definition, but one should make for continuity in thought so far as possible. First get distinctions that are simple, and so far as possible clear, and then show how widely they can be applied to co-ordinate matters apparently different. If your distinctions are not clear and valid, they will not help to bring things to order, but will make only for confusion. Invalid distinctions are as bad as invalid analogies, as finding that everything is like everything else—an evasion that appeals to many who do not like the pain of exact thinking. This distinction between composition and construction as equivalent to the distinction between the poetic and the prosaic is I believe, valid, and I think that it is far-reaching in its power to simplify and illuminate. There are many grades and kinds of the poetic, as I shall go on to show.

Take a baseball game. Structurally a motion picture would record it. Everybody is just what he is and does just what he does, but for the individual spectator this is not at all the case. When the team for which he is rooting makes a play, when his particular hero hits a home run, the whole field is distorted by his interests. It doesn't make at all the same kind of a composition in his mind as when the hated enemy has done the thing. And when he yells himself hoarse, what is he doing but singing a song of victory? It isn't very musical, nor is it organized. When a college crowd gives their college yell it is more so, when they sing their college song it is yet more so, and one can imagine that they might have a cheer leader who, like a Welsh bard, would improvise a song of victory to which the crowd would sing in chorus. Then there would be no doubt that the proceeding was poetic.

The distortion of the scene in the mind of the spectator would also be certified if the teams engaged a painter to make a picture of a certain moment in the play. The picture that would be "true" for one team would be quite false for the other. Interest of the pictorial kind always distorts. I am now looking out on hills a little misty, yellow-greenish-brown, with a milky blue-gray clouded sky beyond, growing more densely white in quiet cumulous cloud, and then a pale-blue sky arching upward to a blue a shade more ultramarine. Nearer is a hill olive-covered, its green-browns dense, and nearer yet single olive trees, whose black-green is nearly metallic in luster. All this varied material is for me so amazingly one, that it is hard to believe that it was not made to be so—it is so "right." It is always so. The spectator at the ball game does not think that he is composing his private picture of the game; he does it as spontaneously as I compose this landscape, which no one else who happens to look in that direction sees as I do.

No object of composition, that is, no work of art, exists in the absence of a spectator. Of course this spectator may be the artist himself. We commonly speak of a book of poems, of poems being printed, but in literal fact a poem cannot be printed. All that can be put in print are indications of a poem that is to come into existence when a reader applies himself to it. One person tries it and there comes out a poem; another tries it and there is no such result. He says it doesn't scan. He says it tells about the unemployed and how if they can't get jobs they'll up and bust things. He says he's read that in the papers a lot of times. Do you call that poetry? Of course it isn't. It happened that the other man read something different from what this man reads; the words were the same but with the same words he made a composition where this man reads merely matters of fact. He reads the words structurally: it says so and so. The other man put them together so as to mean more and other. A composition is of necessity an interpretation, while constructive reading is a mere record.

I have tried again and again the experiment of reading poems by the greatest poets and in various languages in such a way that the accent falls on the merely factual, and at once they cease to be poems or to sound like poems. One doesn't change the place of a word, and one doesn't destroy the meter. What one destroys is the composition. I have not only tried it for myself, I have tried it on others, and always with the same effect. The meter is an essentially structural thing, a kind of trellis on which the composition is stretched, but the composition makes the poem.

A really satisfactory demonstration of this can only be made by reading aloud, and so the reader had best make experiments for himself. However, something can be suggested in print, as the following will show. In *Paradise Lost,* Milton calls on the muse to sing (1) Of man's first disobedience (2) and the fruits of that forbidden tree (3) whose mortal taste brought death into the world (4) and all our woe (5) with loss of Eden (6) till one greater man restore us (7) and regain the blissful seat. If one reads this, noting the itemizing numbers, though not pronouncing them (which would spoil the meter) one will have turned the poem into an inventory without having changed a word or modified the meter.

The poetic never has as its objective the statement of a fact, however many facts it states. There is always reference to an interest that goes beyond that fact in the observer's experience. The man who roots for the ball team of his town is not doing it merely because it is that team, or even because it is the team of his town, but in the last analysis because it is *his* team. He exults in victory. A more impartial man may enjoy a good play, no matter whose, because he exults in felicity of action. Shelley didn't get excited because a little brown bird flies into the air twittering its little note, but because he had aspirations and longings and hopes that he could concentrate on it. The lyric form of his poem has as its basis the composition of a world of meanings around a little bird that is attending to its own business. The poets for the most part say everything about the swallow except that it swallows, which is the real structural reason for those marvellous gyrations which have caused it to be central to so many compositions. Structurally man is just one of the facts in the universe, but compositionally he is its center. *His* feelings, *his* desires, *his* hopes cause him to arrange things so that he can get at least a moment's satisfaction from these interests. If he gets from them the satisfactions as though he had altered the world of real things beyond the periphery of his inner life, he is sentimentally, pathologically falsifying the world, and confusing the realms of poetry and prose.

It is difficult to avoid this anthropomorphosis, perhaps impossible to avoid it altogether, but this is what progressively happens as man becomes more civilized through science. I rather think that when psychology has become an effective science to the degree that physical science is today, the function of art will be the creation of beauty in a much more exclusive sense than it is today. But much time and many revolutions will have occurred before we come to that.

Just as what passes as poetry becomes prosaic when factually taken, so what is mainly prose becomes poetic when it becomes symbolic—with its terms taken in more complex relations. Oratory is full of this. Webster's peroration to his reply to Hayne is obviously poetical, but so too is his simple request at the beginning that Foot's resolution be read. Foot's resolution was nothing to the purpose, but the pause created by it before the storm burst was, and that was composition. Of course the main purpose of the speech was practical, that is, structural—to bring about real changes in the world. But that has been the purpose of much of the serious poetry both of the past and present. The poet as a poet is not a moralist, but most important poets have been moralists as well, and there is no good reason why those who are more interested in morals than in poetry should not read them for this. Really, verse is just a scheme of speech and can serve prosaic purposes extremely well at times. Its mnemonic function is familiar, for everyone knows that it is easier to remember verse than prose. Therefore, when reading and writing were less common than they are today, it was usual to express in verse a lot of things—such as advice to farmers—that today would be written down. I read the other day quite a long bit of writing in verse of a social political kind, which I thought gained by being written in verse, as the short lines simplified and emphasized the points the author was making. The insistence that verse be, before all, poetic is a mere prejudice, a convention, an arbitrary principle of classification.

The most prosaic utterances can become poetic in a composition of meanings. The Italians say "Quatt' quatt' otto" (four and four make eight) to mean that things are what they are and will be what they will be. These simple words are charged with the crack of doom. Their structural meaning is arithmetical, but compositionally their force lies in the contrast between that summary condensation and the immensity of significance. This is accentuated by cutting down the two syllables of "quattro" to a single one. One cannot find a more emphatic illustration of the difference between construction and composition. "Prose" and "poetry" are nouns, and "poetic" and "prosaic" are adjectives. Adjectives qualify nouns. Poetry, it has often been said in one form or another, is mostly a matter of nouns. There are many ways to say this—as that poetry is pictorial, that it points at things rather than describes them, that it is a calling them names, and so on. But these particular names are not essential; they are symbolic of values implicit in them. Hamlet was a prince of Denmark. He might just as well have been a prince of any other place or no prince at all. Romeo and Juliet by any other name, place or station, would have been as sweet. What is significant is not the nominal but the adjectival, not the particular but the quality. *Poetry is adjectives expressed in nouns,* the abstract of values expressed in the concrete of terms.

For purposes of prose, words mean exactly their literal reference. We may call a horse an equine quadruped, or use any other synonym, but the other term must be a synonym. Shelley and Wordsworth were not so restricted, and could call the skylark and the daisy anything they pleased because the structural function of these beings was merely to serve a compositional purpose in another structure of moral significance that again was never made explicit (as in a moral treatise), but was full of implications. To develop this, some examples are at hand.

The structural character of the personages in Romeo and Juliet is characteristically firm. If Romeo and Juliet had lived, they would have proved thoroughly competent members of society—Juliet exceptionally so. She would have been a perfect chatelaine, and this definiteness of character is true of almost everyone in the play. The nature of the language fits them. Despite its rhetoric, the language is solidly factual; Shakespeare's words, even in this early play, have the value of things. A work of art is successful when structure and composition concur, when what is intended and what is said go well together. The firmness of the figures and the firmness of the language are perfectly concordant. Of course, besides being successful, the play is interesting and splendid—though a work of art may be successful and still not be interesting, be successful and not be a success.

Compare the realism of Romeo and Juliet with the diaphaneity of the *Eve of St. Agnes*. This also is a successful work of art, also interesting, and in it Keats tells the same story. There is a lover, a beloved maiden, the rival houses, the feast, a nurse, a priest, but everything else how different! When the lovers go out into the storm, they disappear forever. Beyond the poem they are not viable. There is a structure there, and a firm one, but of moving figures of an exquisite but blended outline. The language is in perfect keeping, the language of high poetry:

A casement high and triple-arched there was
All garlanded with carven imag'ries
Of fruit and flowers and bunches of knot-grass,
And diamonded with panes of quaint device,
Innumerable of stains and splendid dyes
As are the tiger-moth's deep-damasked wings

—and so on. The stuff and the language are admirably concordant in the poem.

Take another case: the fairy tale and the ballad, the poetry of the lowly. Everything is factually stated; the unreal is realistic both as to material and language, and again concordant, once more successful art.

There are many ways in which composition can fail in relation to structure. For the critics of the Romantic period, there was something very objectionable in the eighteenth-century writers' use of artificial language with naturalistic substance. In opposition to this, Wordsworth invented a dogma of common language as false as what he opposed. Fortunately, in practice, he did like most good artists, who are better in their work than in their thinking about it; he wrote good poetry in spite of his theories. In both of these cases, it was a matter of a kind of medium. Often the failure is not of this sort, but is a failure to express adequately what is intended. The poetical anthologies are a choice of the successful compositions, those rare moments of perfection where a structure of sense has come to life in the perfect selection of compositional means. Such perfection is rare, and much critical attention is put upon the failure in great matter or the failure to make it effective.

To some the notion of composition may seem insufficiently important for so lofty a theme as poetry, because they think of poetry only in terms of the final emergent product. But such a person does not realize sufficiently that the act of composition is definitively creative, whether it happens spontaneously or with great labor. The composer makes the choice of just those values in his experience which are compositional rather than structural, which are the things not with isolated meanings but which lend themselves most readily to interpenetration, to integration. Max Eastman insists on the poetic value of certain words. To this I agree. He says that "ruddy" is a poetic word. It is. It is also compositionally active. It means a ruddy apple, a ruddy cheek. If one compares it with "red," one easily sees a difference. Cheeks are red and so are apples. But equally red are ochres and one end of the spectrum. "Ruddy" chooses its associates as "red" does not. The great poetical interests demand compositional expression, while the unpoetic, the calculable, the measurable things are satisfied with words that connect but do not compose.

Of the poetic substance Hazlitt has spoken forcibly. He says, "Fear is poetry, hope is poetry, love is poetry, hatred is poetry; contempt, jealousy, remorse, admiration, wonder, pity, despair, or madness, all are poetry." Hazlitt's statement is extravagant, since the feelings are not poetry, but simply its occasion. But they are specially the occasion of it because they are qualitative, not specific and definable things. Action because of them may be the stuff of poetry, but only appreciation of them grounds poetry.

There is a rule of Latin grammar that smacks of the poetical. It concerns words that take the dative, words signifying favor, help, please, trust and their contraries; also believe, persuade, command, obey, serve, resist, envy, threaten, pardon, spare. The poetic quality of an epigram, of Pope's couplets, of proverbs, lies in large part in their persuasiveness. There is a rapture great or little as they hit the mark. A hit, a palpable hit! For this we forbear to inquire into the limitations of their truth.

The analytic and the measurable are not, as such, apt for composition, but for construction, and are not poetic. Neither is the instrumental. Milton wrote in Lycidas:

I come to pluck your berries harsh and crude
And with forced fingers rude
Shatter your leaves before the mellowing year.

Quiller-Couch, in the *Oxford Book of English Poetry*, is guilty of a comma after "rude." As rightly printed, shattering with forced fingers is qualitative and poetical; the offensive comma puts an emphasis on the instrumental. One can imagine some teacher using this text asking the awful question, "With what did Milton shatter the leaves" and the docile pupil answering that it was "with forced fingers rude." One could also imagine a modern poet writing forced-finger-rudely-shattering, and that is the right sense. Punctuating for the constructive is a process of articulating, but for composition it is a means for unity.

I have said that many bits of the Bible that Henley wisely puts among lyrics, Pearsall Smith and Quiller-Couch put among prose selections. Yet it is certain that verse is more commonly recognized as poetic than prose is. I have also said that anything, at least any complete sentence, can be made poetic or prosaic according as we stress the constructive or the compositional. The orator, the preacher, the auctioneer, the lawyer addressing a jury, would not read even an itemized list the way a clerk or a statistician does. The latter wants to make the items naked; the others want them to have implications, meanings beyond what is said outright. The better they succeed in the dressing of the mere constructional material, the more this is transfigured and suffused with values not its own. The speakers vary the additions as they wish to persuade, command or threaten, to please or horrify. They are variously and in various degrees poetical. To be sure, their ultimate object is a practical result, and in so far they are instrumental; but most poets are also in their degree preachers, even the poets of today. It happens strangely that the greatest of poets has no "message," but Shakespeare is an exception among poets of importance. Disinterestedness is not at all common.

Verse is the most generally applicable of all the means to dispose people to a relatively small concern with what is constructive. Bacon said, "Prosperity is the blessing of the Old Testament, adversity is the blessing of the New." I am no poet, but as I dwell on this sentence of Bacon's I feel myself swelling with a poetic afflatus. But on the other hand, as I think about it, I remember that there are both earlier and later prophets, that the New Testament also promises eventual bliss to those parted on the right side. There is a measure of truth in it, but it is not at once clear how much truth. If instead of a sentence from Bacon, this had been a poem on that subject by Milton, I should have been less inclined to consider the measure of this truth. Milton says that *Paradise Lost* should justify the ways of God to man. I sometimes find the arguments tedious, but I never stop to think whether they are valid or not, though Dr. Johnson did. Verse has obvious compositional appeal, and disposes the reader to confidence. It may satisfy him that it meant more than he can find in it, or may even content him with its suggestion of significance when he can find no definite meaning.

Many years ago in the Woods Hole Laboratory mess I heard a boy and girl talk about poetry. The boy said how strange it was that some most beautiful poetry was quite without meaning. The girl agreed, "Like Shelley's lovely lines, 'Life like a dome of many-colored glass, stains the white radiance of eternity.' " Prose most easily impresses as compositional when it is markedly rhythmic, like that of Sir Thomas Browne, Jeremy Taylor, De Quincey, Ruskin, though some of the most perfect of all prose which is full of poetic significance, like that of Lamb and Emerson, is not so obviously rhythmical. But in much prose writing a direction of attention to compositional values will bring out more than is at first apparent. We are accustomed to reading prose without this attention to all the words which is essential to appreciation of composition. We skim off the meaning and are satisfied with that. We take it for granted that the prose writer wishes us to be concerned with what he talks about, that he is referential, pointing away from the form to the content, while what is written in verse has an existential quality and is taken for its own sake. This may not be the case at all. The writer of prose is at times as much interested in the value of every word as the verse writer, but few readers share this interest.

Emerson's essays can admirably illustrate the way the prosaic and poetic interpenetrate. I find in reading him that there are constant variations. Passages occur which I spontaneously take as poetry, passages which may even have been for Emerson quite literal. For him the idealism was fact, while for me it is only symbolic. But then I come on sentences of shrewd criticism which I take factually. Often a passage first read is taken prosaically, it tells something, but when the sense has become familiar this is easily taken up into the immediacy of the whole and acts mainly to contribute substance to a whole whose value is poetical. It is often best at first to read a difficult poem as though it were prose and gradually to let its literal meaning become absorbed into the tissue of the poetic whole which is veritably the poem.

It is a commonplace, not a very clever commonplace, that art is at bottom emotional—that it is the expression of the emotions. This may have seemed satisfactory once upon a time, when in despite of all the evidence, man was thought to be the rational animal. Today that illusion is lost. We accept now what people in practice always knew—that it is by emotional appeals that men are stirred to action, that emotion is found almost everywhere except in pure logic. Since emotion is found everywhere, and not merely in art, it has little value as a definition. But since in order to make emotion practically effective it must for the most part make people think it is something else, the prose form which disguises it is more effective. For propaganda therefore, in our literate age, we do not use verse as it was used when ears were more important than eyes. The famous assertion of Fletcher of Saltoun that "if a man is permitted to make all the ballads he need not care who made the laws of the nation" had ceased to have any application when newspapers took the place of ballads, though now "the radio voice" and radio style are once more making ears important. The intervening period has, however, attuned us to prose propaganda and that is the form continued even for aural consumption.

A great advantage of this notion of the compositional and the constructive is that we need never bother to decide whether any work is poetry or prose. We have simply to read it and get out of it what we can or what we are disposed to. We can stress this or that. If it have not the values we desiderate, we need not object to others finding what they want. Because we have decided that it is some kind of thing, is no good reason to accuse those who take it otherwise of taking it wrongly. Wordsworth wrote in *The Prelude* one of the most interesting of all autobiographies. Much of it is just prose written in verse form, utterly blank verse with occasional Miltonic frills; much of it is good passages of magnificent, unquestionable poetry. *The Prelude* is a great book; it is not certainly a great poem. If one accepts my position, one reads ahead for the interest of whatever kind that is found, prosaic or poetic, and makes no protest because what is written ought to be this or that. The field is not dogmatically narrowed. The artist is a man who claims to do as he likes. Sometimes he admits to limits, sometimes to very narrow limits, but he insists that they be self-imposed, that they be not legislation imposed by another. Critics like to classify and have often been dictatorial. They have taken what has been done as a rule for what should be done. They like demarcations, and don't like to be disturbed by an obligation to remove their frontier marks. They often think that to be inevitable which is not inevitable at all. The poetic and the prosaic have both always been present in all literature, and much is gained by breaking through the conventions that ignore this.

In 1908 Minkovski said that "from this hour space of itself and time of itself sink to mere shadows and only a blend of the two retains an independent existence." Minkovski could appeal to mathematics to justify what he said. Without mathematics, I hold it reasonable to say the same thing of the prosaic and the poetic. As we read literature, whether in verse or prose form, and move lightly or heavily through a sea of this common quality, we experience now more, now less, of one or the other value. Neither is ever entirely absent, though either may for the time be ignored. Pure time becomes timeless, pure space is empty even of space, and so it is with prose and poetry.

IV

Appreciation

It is not only obvious, it is known to all that art is not primarily to give information or to serve practical ends. It can be opposed to science and utility, but since emotional conduct and rational conduct are no longer contrasted sharply, it is no longer useful to call art the expression of the emotions. As one needs a term for that with which art is concerned, I propose the word appreciation. It is a word quite free from misleading associations and is, I think, relevant.

The word is not to have a technical meaning. It will be used in a sense that is sufficiently usual to make it readily understood. It means taking things for values found in them directly, and not as the result of analysis. Analysis may, of course, be used for purposes of preliminary study, to prepare for a more intimate acquaintance; but appreciation always deals with wholes.

Though art depends on appreciations, appreciations serve many other purposes than art. We use appreciations of people to judge capacities that are not susceptible to accurate testing. The ordinary person does very little precise analysis, and uses almost everywhere in his daily affairs the method of appreciation—sniffing, tasting, pushing, pulling, feeling, comparing. His sensibilities are trained by practice, and for a new situation he feels the relevancies, rather than knowing them objectively. So it is that most people more or less successfully make their way through life.

Science and appreciation are often in competition with each other, and the less there is of science the more is the dependence on appreciation. Metal seekers, dowsers, witch doctors who smelt out the cause of ills, were all acting appreciatively. The family doctor, so highly prized, whose diagnosis both physical and mental was a sensitive perception rather than a systematic analysis, was appreciative rather than scientific. Until recently our best authorities for characterology were novelists and not psychologists. Only in the last few years, since Freud and Simon-Binet, has this begun to change.

It is the same with law. We still depend for judgment in criminal and civil cases on the appreciations of juries and judges. There are such things as lie detectors, and I have heard that there is a hypnotic drug which makes it possible to get truthful replies to questions. The time will doubtless come when it will be seen that the serious business of life should be settled by methods where the concern for truth is primary, and should not be left to duels between clever people whose object is the evasion of truth. But in fact the interest in truth is as yet very slight, and it will be long before it becomes much greater.

Man is the most confused of all animals. He has certain impulses, tendencies, instincts, it is hard to say what they had best be called, which can never come to action in a pure state. Insects are born full grown as adults, and other animals in varying degrees are independent of education; but man is so largely made by it that we can come to no exact idea of what he would be without it. What concerns me here is that appreciations are determined by a lot of things entirely unrecognized, that men feel that they are acting inevitably and in accordance with their essential nature, thinking that they are peculiarly themselves, when in fact they are merely conventional, and expressing what their education, and not anything essentially themselves, forces them to. Man does not know what impels him, and so he easily takes himself for granted and is to a comical degree the center of the universe. I do not mean man as a species, but the individual person. Of course he does not assert this in so many words, but he thinks and acts as though it were true.

Whene'er I take my walks abroad
How many poor I see,
What shall I render to my God
For all his gifts to me.

It is the pious Dr. Watts who speaks. Though a good

and charitable man, he has a peculiarly tender feeling for himself. God is of course the God of the poor as well as of Dr. Watts, but God's relation to the poor is not exactly the same as it is to the pious doctor. If instead of blessings it were afflictions that rained upon him, it would be the same. He would always be the center of things.

All men feel this way more or less, but the artist makes of this peculiar position his stock in trade. His business is not to inquire into the validity of his feelings but to exploit them, to paint the universe, or as much of it as he can grasp, from the particular angle of his private perspective. Dr. Watts, if accused of this personal position, would have denied it, but the artist glories in it. The artist tends to believe that his private vision is insight, is the perception of truth in some way beyond that of the average man. He is to some extent the seer or prophet. Therefore the extravagant claims he so often makes for his business. Nothing is more fantastic than poets on poetry, of which Shelley's essay is a famous example. "Poetry, and the principle of self, of which money is the visible incarnation, are the God and Mammon of the world. . . . Poetry is indeed something divine. It is at once the center and circumference of knowledge; it is that which comprehends all science and that to which all science must be referred."

This notion of the poet's authority derives really from the felt validity of instinct, but ignores the possibility of error. Instinct is indeed infallible if the conditions for its exercise are invariable. Instinct is like a machine made to work under precisely given conditions. There can be no failure if the conditions are in all respects observed. If no sands get into the bearings, if the materials fed into it are of the kind and the quality intended, if the handling is right, the product is assured. But the more complex the conditions become, the more varied the uses, the more the machine is fallible.

What is true of the machine is true of the living thing. Instinct will sufficiently serve the bee and the ant; it will less competently serve man. The poet, like the religiously inspired, does not reckon with these possibilities of error. He sees as an individual and believes in himself as an individual. As an individual he *knows* because he appreciates. He is like the religious believer, a man of faith who knows that God is on his side, that he must be somehow right if he expresses himself—not right only in his expression, but also in his insight.

The scientific temper is not adjusted to this mania of egocentricity. One deals then with the individual as a member of the class, as representing a kind. If God really bore the same relation to everybody that he does to me, he would be a great deal less interesting, for then others would be as right as I am. If good or bad can befall everybody on exactly the same conditions as they befall myself, then God can with difficulty be given a sympathetic character. One does not define this but one feels it.

Some pious Catholic friends thought I ought to be grateful to God because I had during the German occupation and the fascist republic escaped all perils. I said to them that there had been six million Jews murdered. Was I to be grateful to God that only six million had been murdered and not six million and one? I do not see how anyone can have this quaint combination of grateful humility and massive conceit without being in some way profoundly stupid. People will not surrender their private claims. So there is a strange incapacity to see that they are only people, that their feelings of themselves (which are entirely legitimate for many things) have gathered up facts of experience which happen in the indifferent world of things, and twisted them into the fiber of themselves so that they come to believe they are dealing with realities of the objective world. They rely on their appreciations, which are naively taken as descriptions of a real world.

Once upon a time, in the age of faith so much extolled by some, confusion between appreciation and factual reality was more openly acceptable than it is today. When St. Anselm was stopped on the coast of France by a storm, and so prevented from hurrying on to England, he asked himself why God should have done this thing. He then remembered a vow to pray before a certain shrine, and when he had done this the storm abated. He was not concerned about the others who were also held up by the storm, for—to his feelings, not, of course, to his intellect—God was his God. When someone, Mark Twain, I think, saw the levees burst because of the floods just when he had relapsed after a boyhood conversion, he felt that it was because of him that the catastrophe had come. Of course he later knew that this was silly. For Anselm the objective fact never came to be so separate from the personal feeling as it did for the later man, who did not belong to the age of faith. People are still innocent enough to believe that there is some interposition serving their personal or group fortunes though, of course, this must happen somehow without disturbing the laws of nature. God will look out for them or their factions or sects or country, though natural law still rules everything else.

This kind of feeling, so natural to the artist, whose intuition assures him that he has his finger on the pulse of Truth, has suffered a serious diminution of range through science. Science accepts the reality of the instincts and the validity of their impulses. Just as "the wisdom of the body" is shown by its adjustments to maintain temperature and nutrition, so man acts to preserve his life and his mind. But to a constantly greater extent in contact with a diversified world, he comes to recognize that what once upon a time was supposed to be known was really imagined, and that the real facts are very different. From Galileo on, the physical world has more and more become a world in which the poet feels less perfectly at home. The poets painfully lamented the intrusion of the scientist. Thus Keats:

Do not all charms fly
At the mere touch of cold philosophy?
There was an awful rainbow once in heaven:
We know her woof, her texture, she is given
In the dull catalogue of common things.
Philosophy will clip an angel's wings,
Conquer all mysteries by rule and line,
Empty the haunted air and gnomed mine,
Unweave the rainbow.

And Wordsworth:

Physician art thou?—one all eyes,
Philosopher! a fingering slave,
One that would peep and botanize
Upon his mother's grave?

And to him he opposes one

with modest looks
And clad in homely russet brown.
He murmurs near the running brooks
A music sweeter than their own. . . .
But he is weak, both man and boy,
Hath been an idler in the land;
Contented if he might enjoy
The things that others understand.

Wordsworth is not doing himself justice; he thought that he really understood them a great deal better, that the poet's understanding was real in some enormous sense beyond that of the nasty physician and philosopher—natural philosopher, of course.

It has now come to pass that the poet leaves to the man of science the understanding of the physical world, that here he is without pretensions. But he still tends to believe that somehow his vision is something more than a private matter. A private matter, yes, but which ought to be valid for others also. After all, how does it come about that anything can be so truly whole unless it be also somehow true? He fails to see that what is whole is self-contained, has its own validity, is a little cosmos with its own constitution and laws, no matter how eccentric it is to common experience—

that it is of necessity right and final because it is a cosmos. It is a creation, a kind of reality, and it is justified because of this. Its relations to the worlds outside itself, and therefore its effectual worth to the larger world, cannot be judged from the limited standpoint of its creator. For this there is needed a view of the complex relations that connect the individual experience of the artist with experiences of others. It is this sort of thing that the philosophical critic considers. Of course he cannot be a final judge because he too has his limited point of view, but at least he has the merit, if at all competent, to see the problem and to try for a more comprehensive solution.

The critic today has some advantage over the critic of a former day, inasmuch as modern psychology has since Freud become the psychology of the individual, and has ceased to ape the physical sciences, which it could not resemble. As yet it has done very little, but it has done enough to make the problem clearer, to make more certain that the poet's insight is not a guarantee of truth, that the real function of the artist, his intrinsic function, is to satisfy the need for totality, which he serves by creating individual worlds, little cosmoses which satisfy the hunger for wholeness as food satisfies the body's need for restoration, though only the eventual process of assimilation can show what food was really nourishing.

The total method of art is of necessity opposed to the analysis of science. The wholes of art deny anything but a suggestive analysis. The elements of which these wholes are made resist analysis because they lack independence. In the synthesis of science the units remain unique through all the transformations. Hydrogen elements and oxygen elements put in certain relations to each other have, as a result, water with its emergent properties, which are different from those of the gases; but the atoms in the new molecules do, for the scientist, retain completely their identity. The philosopher of organism may insist that this analysis of the scientist is not sufficient, that really the atoms in a molecule, the electrons in an atom, cannot be exactly what they are when not so related, but the philosopher is not a scientist, rather a kind of poet who deals with imponderables. The scientist is concerned with what can be measured and weighed; he cannot deal with imponderables.

The artist is he who deals with imponderables, and as artist, specifically, with nothing else. In this he is different not only from the scientist but also from the constructor. In construction every element occupies its particular place and is externally related to the other elements. In an arch, for instance, constructively taken, the stones of the base support those next to them and so on up to the keystone, but if we take the arch compositionally, the stones of the bases are related to every other stone in the arch and to every particular point in them.

In a composition every element deforms its neighbor. There is a kind of fusion, an interpenetration, an action at a distance, and not merely a neighborhood relation between the words of a poem or the colors of a picture. One can often show that, if a word is changed or a color altered, there is not merely a difference in meaning but that everywhere within the present field of attention there are changes which are utterly incapable of analysis. When Chevreul, the famous French chemist whose work started the impressionists on their color novelties, showed a manufacturer that his failure to get certain blacks was due to his neglect of complementaries, he was pointing to something which could be analyzed. But Cézanne, with his famous spots (on the hand in a portrait) which were left blank because if he put in the wrong thing the whole picture would go wrong, was concerned with something that could not be analyzed. The manufacturer wanted a certain black to be locally black and not grayish. That could be stated in general terms. But Cézanne wanted a complex whole to satisfy an indefinable demand. If the right color was put in the place he could *see* that all was right, and if it was the wrong color he could *see* that all was wrong. A lot of indefinable relations were involved.

Another excellent illustration occurs in the composition of Keats's most famous lines. He wrote:

> *And magic casements opening on the foam*
> *Of ~~keelless~~ perilous seas in faery lands forlorn.*

His first thought, "keelless" was imaginatively fine, much finer than "perilous," but the movement was not effective nor the volume of sound. If "keelless" had been left, the lines might have seemed fine to those who paused over the meaning, but they would not have been the familiar lines that they have become. The inferiority in meaning was more than compensated for by the formal splendor caused by the included dactyl.

Though science and art are so essentially different, they are both important to us, even though the kinds of importance are not equally clear. The importance of science of one kind or another is never questioned, not even by the most barbarous of peoples. Everybody wants to have things explained, even little children. There have been many civilizations for which science meant a sort of religious cosmology, and for these the distinction of art and science was not at all definite. It was only when science began to be rigorous, when measurements commenced to be exact, and accurate verification was demanded, that the split became irreconcilable. Then art had to find another justification than that which before had been sufficient.

In our time there has come about a change such as the world never before saw. The extension of scientific range in application is equaled by its extension in the popular consciousness. It is the first time in history that everybody is actively aware of it. The resistance is great. Science means the reign of law, and "free" people don't like so much law. Art is, by contrast, a world of freedom, where one can believe what one likes and can be "proved" wrong only by the negligible critic. Every time a so-called bankruptcy of science occurs, shouts of joy and thanksgiving go up. The strait jacket that confines the spirit is ripped, and man once more is free. The latest instance is the Heisenberg indetermination, which calls to question the legitimacy of science's pet child, causality. The will is free, and anyone can believe anything one likes. Of course all the real causalities that man is faced with remain the same. Fire still burns and ice still freezes. What the new doctrines mean is not easy to understand, but there is none the less the pleasure of release, the triumph over a remorseless enemy.

Despite these successes of the free spirit, art remains something of an outsider. No one can question it as an amusement, as an excitant, as a diversion for one's leisure time. But the inclination of man today is not to be satisfied with this conception. The feeling is that art has some vital function, and that it should be taken seriously, even in the universities. But when one reads what is written in favor of this view one generally finds it unconvincing. My own impression is that the concept of appreciation helps.

To appreciate one must apprehend, must in some sense get hold of things massively. Man, like all animals, wants food, shelter, sex-satisfaction; like all higher animals, he wants acquaintance with the world about him. The satisfactions in appreciation are massive satisfactions, and they belong essentially not to the satisfactions of the higher but of the lower senses: taste, smell, touch, the orgasmic. These are also the senses more especially related to the instincts of animals.

To pass over from them to the higher senses, there was necessary, I think, binocular vision—by which a combination of spatial order and spatial unity was made possible. Binocular vision is a means of isolation. It separates things from their backgrounds, and so gives them individual existence. In this way a composite visual field and a consequent auditory one were made distinctly available. Then by rhythmic movements dependent on man's bipedal balance, in walk, developing into march and dance (perhaps the earliest art expressions) this massive whole came to be articulated, and the world of appreciations became the world of art.

Appreciations remain basic, felt wholes of experience. At an early period these wholes were little individualized. They were tribal interests, religious and social, and not much varied in kind. But with the development of individuality, their range extended, till now anything is included that anyone appreciates in any way. No matter how far the appreciations are altered and developed by increase of intellectual and spiritual interests, the basic massive primitive qualities remain. Without them there is neither rhythm nor form, nor the mysterious quality of indeterminate great value.

There is, of course, a great difference between authentic primary and conventional secondary appreciations. The respect and regard for the classics are mostly of this second kind. People who have no direct contact with these believe in them because they are told to do so—not directly perhaps, but by all sorts of purposed and incidental propaganda. What I am now considering is the real kind, which for some has as its object a Bach, a Holbein or a Donne, and for others the crassest of best sellers. Admitting that the satisfaction in appreciation is deep seated, we may still ask what there is in art that answers to this demand. To illustrate the intensity of this feeling for art I shall give an example.

I once wanted to buy a Renoir which was costly, and for this purpose I sold other pictures. I had a little Renoir, a nude woman standing knee deep in water with her arms over her head. A certain collector liked it and had asked me to let him know if I ever wished to get rid of it. So I wrote him saying that I needed a certain sum, and if he was ready to pay that much I would sell the picture. There had been something in the movement of one arm that disturbed the whole, but as I looked at the picture after I had written the letter, the arm suddenly came right. I was in a panic. Before me was an extraordinary picture that I had not yet seen. To lose it now would be a disaster. Much as I wanted the other picture, which was much finer, I couldn't face the absence of this one. I sent a cable message, saying that the offer in the letter was withdrawn. Only after some weeks, when I had fully assimilated the picture in its new aspect, were negotiations renewed, and eventually I did get the other one. Why this so serious reaction to a little painting of a woman standing in the water with her arms over her head *only* when it came just right?

I think this is due in large part to the completion, the rounding out of certain movements started within. These meet something outside which seems to make the experience absolute. The most obvious instance is sex. Sex is the most common occasion of art, either expressly or by implication, and the sexual object is for most people the one unquestionable beauty. The internal organic impulse to seek its object is here the strongest, and that object is the most enticing. Man and woman become one flesh even before they are in one another's arms.

What is true of sex is true for all sensory objects which are desired, and this can be extended also to ideas—for those to whom ideas have sufficient reality. If men and women came together too spontaneously they would not have occasion to find beauty in each other, but the preliminary period of courtship gives this opportunity. So it is with other things, which must be seen, handled, tasted, before being finally utilized. For most people the interest in beauty is not strong enough as an impulse from within to become operative. It needs the stimulus of an object already prepared to wake them up. The artist is specifically the person who has this impulse. He also is the one who enlarges to the utmost the range of completions. His attention goes out to things that the common person finds without attraction of any kind. The important thing in all this is that the object should be at once absorbed and remain self-existent, like the beloved man or woman. When objects so assimilated still remain separate existences, still have existential character—though only in memory, as food once eaten and digested can still be enjoyed—we are in the world of art, the world of so-called esthetics.

Beauty can in general be conceived in terms of this kind. Beauty, I should say, is the extension of the organic over the heterogeneous, or—reversed—the integration of the heterogeneous into the organic. This sounds a bit portentous, but simply means that the world of fact is complex and various, and that appreciation orders it in response to an organic demand on our part. What is already organic is most easily apprehended as beautiful: men, animals, birds, flowers, plants; then things that are pseudo-organic, like crystals and geometric forms; then the picturesque; and finally everything which an imaginative effort can subdue to our organic requirements.

There is also a kind of art which concerns objects having less of this existential value. One might call it the art of environment, the art which one does not focally attend to, but which one feels as making for an ambient delight. Decorative art is of this kind. I once visited a Frenchman who had an important collection of Renoirs. His living room was charming, and as we sat over a cup of tea, I noticed that a clock on the mantelpiece was very fine. This led me to look more particularly at other things, and I saw that everything was good. He told me how this had happened.

He was a mining engineer who came home with a fortune. He was a widower, and for distraction he furnished his apartment with slow and serious care. He spent several years in this way, insisting that everything should be good and should enter into the scheme of the whole. Then he thought he ought to have some pictures. He knew nothing about pictures but he knew Renoir, had known him since they were children. So he went to Renoir for pictures and advice. He got more and more Renoirs, for it is a peculiarity of Renoir's pictures that they enhance each other, and make decorative wholes. His pictures, like his furniture, were individually good and fitted in their places. One room whose walls were covered with a yellow silk was difficult, and for a while he thought he would have to change the walls, but he finally found that a certain type of Renoir went admirably on it. If I had not noticed the clock while we were having tea, I might just have looked at the pictures and have missed this interesting adventure.

Works of art happen because some people have a gift for expressing their appreciations in a communicable form, and in consequence of that gift, intensify and extend the range of their attention. It is quite natural that it should come to pass that they fix their appreciations on the work itself rather than on anything else, and so we come to have works of art for art's sake, which might be called the art of immediacy, art which does not mediate between the artist and the world of events, but stops short at itself. This was the art which people for a while thought was to be the art for all those of a higher culture, but things are turning out a little differently.

Propaganda was considered beneath the level of such people, though most of the great art of all times has been more or less propaganda. Homer was the laureate of a warrior class; Dante, Milton, Cervantes, Dickens, Donne, Blake, Virgil, Horace—all were propagandists. Religious painting was propaganda. The appreciations of the artist are for the most part like those of other people; it is only his capacity to explore, intensify and express his appreciations that make him different. For a while it seemed as though there was nothing more of importance for him to say. Then came the present moment, the moment of revolution. Men had felt themselves to be at the end of an epoch, and then discovered that this was only half a truth —that they are also at the beginning of an epoch. A beginning is more encouraging than an end, and it is possible that propaganda will have a new lease of life.

Propaganda can outlive its period of effectiveness as such. Spenser wrote the *Faerie Queene* as a moral discourse in allegorical form. Hazlitt said that "the allegory won't bite you." He was not altogether right, for at times the allegory jumps at you ferociously with a moral platitude, but he was substantially right.

No one today reads Spenser for the moral. But some propaganda is almost eternal—like the fables and the parables of Jesus—and there are characters and events in history, like Caesar and Alexander and Napoleon, the origins of Christianity and the French Revolution, which continually come to life for their propagandistic value. There is other propaganda so short-lived that the occasion is soon forgotten. Occasional poems live beyond their occasion. A well-known Italian historian says that one object of the poems of Horace was to advertise Italian wines when Greek wines were the fashion. I don't know whether this is true, but we all know that when we read Horace we do not notice this.

Propaganda, what one in art wishes to induce, leads naturally to the "art of one's time." Since there are only a few original people in the world, people with fundamentally fresh appreciations and who have their total trend of expression determined by their personal experience, there is more uniformity than one might expect, in view of the large number who think they have something to say. Art is mostly a game of "follow the leader" even when one pretends that one doesn't. There are periods of extreme stylistic uniformity, and periods so little so that there seems to be more originality than is real.

Such is the Jazz Age. It was fortunate in having, among others, Freud to shake up the human insides, and Cézanne to shake up the program of painting. Cézanne did two things; he emphasized color and he simplified forms. There were a lot of close Cézanne imitators, of course, but they were the dullest of the dull. Cézanne, making his appeal by purely compositional qualities, and with a negligible illustrative interest, is satisfying only when the effort is successful. Cézanne had the vision and the patience to pull the thing off, completely now and then, approximately more often.

No one else could do it at all. Therefore the Cézannesque tradition could be made effective only by disaggregation, some using this bit and some that, but leaving the whole high and dry. The world received shock after shock as the disaggregation went on, and finally was afraid to hazard a judgment. They had to say to the artist, "Do as you please," the famous slogan of Rabelais' Abbey of Thélème—and the artist did in fact as he pleased. The readiness of the public to see was pathetic. I once asked a young woman in charge of a museum what she saw in a certain Cézanne which was a hopeless failure, abandoned by the artist when the mess was complete. She said that at first she saw nothing, but by dint of looking she had come to see something. I asked whether she thought she would have been able to see anything if she had not known it was a Cézanne, and she said she thought she would not.

That is the sort of thing that happens when art has been discovered. Someone has to "discover" it if it is a new kind, and then propaganda, which propagates appreciation, is required to make others come to the scratch. I've done some discovering and some propaganda, and know how it happens. One man who came to my place in Paris told me that the only Cézannes he cared for were those he saw there. Certainly they were not the best Cézannes, but the place was charged with the atmosphere of propaganda, and he succumbed.

There are individual appreciations and mass appreciations. Mass appreciations of what the individual couldn't possibly see for himself are rather of the nature of taste than of real appreciation. To be a man of good taste is for the most part to be one subdued to an environment from which one takes color, and if one has been rightly brought up one sees and does the contemporary right thing. As I grew up rather Topsy-like, I was often amazed to see how people in good society showed such excellent judgment when I knew that as individuals they were incapable of any judgment at all in such matters. They knew the right thing, because for them the right thing was not a particular thing, but a kind of thing, and they were conditioned to the kind. To be conditioned to particular appreciations is impossible, because that which is decisive is particular, a whole which differs from others in ways that can be recognized only in the whole—in short, an individual experience, and not an experience of a kind.

What is called the art of the time is not generally what the people of the time appreciate. The art of the time is paradoxically that which only a tiny minority at the moment consider as such, and which even they can't be sure is really the art of the time, that which will be so considered in retrospect. What is taken to be such may be mere scum and froth. Practically, the notion is not of much value, except to the historian. In one's own time the important thing is to know what counts vitally in one's experience, to use the superior people as stimulants to one's attention, but not as authorities, which they aren't. They are just a little herd who have their own herd leaders, a bit more perceptive than the leaders of the bigger herds, but not any more decisive.

What I here say is peculiarly true of today. At no previous time was so much extravagance admissible and such eccentricity permissible. We are in so many ways at the breakdown of a civilization of old and established standing, and so vaguely in view of what is to succeed it, that the future is any man's guess. Therefore one can choose one's costume, and do as one pleases. Everything is legitimate, provided there is a man of talent to try it—for in art there are no known laws, but only conventions. And for the moment, there is no convention except that there shall be none. The only criticism that could be brought against anyone is that he has not succeeded in doing what he has tried to do. But the critic may in any case be wrong, because the painter, the poet, the musician or the architect may be trying to do something different from what the critic decides.

There will probably be a future, despite the atomic bomb. It is not going to arrive tomorrow or the day after; the interim between the present and the future is going to be long and troubled. But I have some impressions on the subject, and as they help to explain what I mean by appreciation, they can serve as a tail to this chapter.

The unconscious has come to be one of the contemporary commonplaces. It is well known that the word refers to two things that are quite different—the primitive unconscious, which means the impulses that put in operation our individual and social life, and the repressed unconscious, made up of things once known but not effectively available. Two purposes of the human animal have always been recognized as primary, self-preservation and sociality. Man defends himself from attack, and man cannot live alone. He must assure his safety, and he needs the companionship of the other sex and also of other persons.

The lower animals defend themselves, defend their families, and—when they are tribal—defend their kind. They also defend their food, and sometimes their feeding places, but that is probably all. The range of man's defensiveness is enormously larger. He defends not only the present but also the past, on which he relies, and the future, for which he hopes. And because of his repressions, he defends a lot of things that he doesn't even think of defending. To appreciate is to enter into sympathetic contact with things, and every act of defense is a limitation of one's sympathy. It makes of appreciations pseudo-appreciations.

It is, of course, possible to approve in judgment what one appreciates only by convention. The intelligent man who can recognize the right thing may be, and often is, a man who is tightly bottled up in his resistances; his catholic acceptances, which generally exclude the eccentric and in consequence often the important, leave him unchanged. Outside a narrow range of vital experience, he is no more than a superior man of taste.

The large possibilities of genuine appreciation are both limited by his resistances and canalized by them. The more one is on the defensive, the less widely can one appreciate. One sniffs heresies and secret offensives. One is restricted to what will pass the "censor." Of course one can still be amiably receptive to lots of things, provided they keep their distance; but this attitude belongs to the realm of good manners rather than to that of vital culture.

The more one reduces one's resistances, the more one releases things from the repressions of the unconscious—the larger will be the range of one's appreciations. I am convinced that Shakespeare's vast range of appreciations was in part a result of his freedom from the tyranny of defense. It is a quality strikingly in evidence in his sonnets. There is in his plaints an almost open impersonality, an objectiveness which is unique. His humility is also one of simple acceptance. He is not on the defensive about anything: religion, politics, ethics. Bunyan, or some other equally moral person, said of a man in the stocks, "There but for the mercy of God sits John Bunyan." Shakespeare might have said of even his absurdest character, "There but because I can see round him sits William Shakespeare." He was too freely superior to need to feel superior.

The world is full of men who are limited to their own way of seeing things, and who can see no vital possibilities elsewhere. They know what is right, what ought to be, because they see clearly, and feel that they see impartially. Of course this is an utter illusion. They read arguments from the other side, and their intelligence may determine them to say that there is something in it—but with that the matter ends. Even if the reasoning seems convincing, it makes no difference. They are like the Jumping Frog of Calaveras; they are natively competent to jump, but are held in place by their resistances, as the frog was held in place by a handful of birdshot. Nothing can change them unless it comes with the devastating force of the new bomb. Outside what they already accept, the world is—in terms of appreciation—merely a play world, and when they are interested in some kind of art not their own, it is merely an elegant amusement.

To amuse, to entertain, to please, is, of course, an important function of appreciation. The scientist not only practices science but also appreciates it; the business man appreciates business; the politician appreciates political manipulation. One appreciates any activity for which one is competent. There is no more rich and satisfying pleasure than the feeling of an understanding appreciation. This is the special value of escapist literature, even the worst. These are things easy to understand, and easy to appreciate, as they are just objectified satisfactions to elementary demands, without involving the reality which would make them difficult with opposing complications. I remember that when, as a child, I read in fairy tales of "their living happily ever after," I felt that to live happily ever after, all in a minute, was very tedious. Such skepticism did not, of course, belong there, but such skepticism does belong to a more serious criticism of appreciation and art.

Everyone knows that the world is in a bad way, that we are at the end of the road which has led from the beginning of organized society to us, and that we must now take a turning. Either the new way must go through the battlefield of civil war or through the ways of a more comprehensive appreciation. As long as people keep to their repressions and resistances, they will refuse to appreciate each other, and will fight desperately for their own. They have an animal and a human right to their own, but as long as that own is made up in part of repressions which determine unchangeable attitudes—religious, social, proprietary—and which ignore the similar unchangeable attitudes of others, there is no way out except to fight it out.

A new age can begin with Freud; though, of course, with him it only begins. It is often complained that this is an age of irrationality, and some dear people look back regretfully to the ages of faith and rationality. They ignore that such rationality could exist only because there was a sufficiently widespread superstitious basis of conviction. The present Pope in November, 1944, addressing a group of Polish soldiers, reminded them that Sigismund III won the battle of Choçim the very day that the head of the Blessed Stanislaus for which he had sent to Rome, crossed the frontiers of Poland. *Post hoc, propter hoc.* A skeptic asks what Stanislaus was doing when Poland was cut to pieces by its neighbors, and when the Nazis murdered millions of Poles, but those who belong to the ages of faith, though they may argue acutely, do not ask embarrassing questions.

When I was young I once met on the train three young priests, who were on their way to America after having finished their studies in Rome. We soon got into discussions on philosophy. They put forth their basic affirmations. I declined to accept them. They varied the statement somewhat, but I continued recalcitrant.

"But how can we argue if you don't accept something?" they asked.

I said, "You want to argue, and I want to investigate. There is an essential difference."

Faith and rationality go well together, so long as your rationality does not question your grounds of faith. A future age of faith will have to be different from those of the past. It will have to be grounded in a human nature cleansed of confusion and contradiction. The dark cellars must be opened to the light, and then one will see to build both society and art on something better than the rubbish on which creeds and much art, especially that of the surrealists, would raise their edifices.

V

On Reading Poetry and Seeing Pictures

ONE FINDS poetry nowhere if there is no poetry within, said Joubert. There is a stanza in a poem by Campion, not ostensibly about the reading of poetry, which admirably puts the matter:

What harvest half so sweet is
As still to reap the kisses
  Grown ripe in sowing?
And straight to be receiver
Of that which thou art giver,
  Rich in bestowing?

One has to match the text with that which meets the text if the text is to amount to much. *"Anch' io sono pittore,"* "I too am a painter," said Correggio when he saw the works of Michelangelo. Correggio could do more than feel a response to the creative activity whose aura came to him from those colossal things; he actually could do something of his own which, if not Michelangelesque, was at least Correggiesque. Most of us cannot, but where this resonance of the "I too am an artist" is completely lacking, there is at least imperfect appreciation.

I can illustrate with a difference in my reactions to the sonnets of Shakespeare and to those in the *House of Life* of Rossetti. With the sonnets of Shakespeare I feel a complete accord. Even those which are full of conceits and which I have to puzzle out, I can meet—if not halfway, at least well along on the road. But many of Rossetti's, though I may understand them, are foreign to me. If I read and reread them often enough, I may get into tune with them, though at the expense of getting a little out of tune with myself. My appreciation of them does not seem intimately mine. However distant a cousin I may be, I feel myself to be of the family of Shakespeare, while in Rossetti I meet an interesting stranger.

Shakespeare has certainly the largest family of anyone since Homer. Almost everybody at all sensitive to literature is related to him. It happened once, while talking with the late Giorgiana King of Bryn Mawr, that I hesitated in something I was saying as though doubtful whether she understood. She said, "That's all right, we belong to the same generation and talk the same language." Though words may be obsolete and meanings sometimes obscure, yet in a more essential sense we talk the language of Shakespeare and he talks ours. Shakespeare I can take neat; I can take him as he stands. But much of Rossetti I must pause upon; I must re-create him by a sort of translation. His language has not the universality of Shakespeare's, but is, so to speak, a dialect. His creations do not, like Shakespeare's, induce a responsive re-creation in every man's mind, but only in those of his own parish.

Creation and re-creation, these are the motives running through this chapter on reading poetry and seeing pictures. Of course these apply to much besides poetry and painting, but my knowledge of other arts is less. I have long been hard of hearing, and music is for me a reverberation from the past—except in so far as I can murmur it to myself, an obviously inadequate rendering of the masterpieces. "Heard melodies are sweet but those unheard are sweeter" may apply to a Mozart, but not to ordinary beings. Anyway, we are to be concerned with creation and re-creation, and the stuff to work on will be mostly literature and painting.

The question why we should be so much in earnest about art and poetry is one that is bound to recur, for it is really a strange thing. We know why we are in earnest about science, because everyone who is not dull wants to know why things happen; he wants a reason for things even though he is for the most part satisfied with flimsy and foolish reasons. We know why people are in earnest about religion, because they are afraid to stand alone in a universe that is as hostile as ours seems to be. The greater the peril the greater the religious interest. The aristocracy, though officially conservative, are more commonly, in their private lives, free-thinkers than people who are less secure. Increases in church-membership and church attendance measure the failures of civilization. One can easily understand why gambling and games are taken seriously, because people in the mass are passionately excited by them. So with the theater and the novel, which are forms of vicarious experience for that which most people cannot get out of life itself. And music is for all the world—savage and civilized, peasant and lord.

Poetry and pictures are not like these things. Everybody likes pictures but pictures of something. Everyone likes jingly verses set to music, but only a few people read poetry with the kind of interest that they show for all the things already mentioned. People commonly run through the great galleries of the world in less time than they spend at the theater in one evening, and they do not often come back. Millionaires who are perfectly indifferent to pictures spend millions on collecting them, and states consider them as among their most precious possessions. Henry McBride told me that the proprietor of the *New York Sun,* who left a large fortune to the Metropolitan Museum, in his monthly meetings with the department editors of his paper had something to say to everyone except the art editor. The motive that leads to these abnormal actions must be a strong one.

Tradition plays a great part. Pictures, statues, verses—all were once much more intimately related to religion, to the state and to social ritual, than they are today. The elder poetry was concerned with important interests, love, glory, conduct. Montaigne quotes the Latin poets on every page, and almost always the reference is a moral one.

The wisdom of the older world was in large part contained in its verse, and the older criticism always insisted on this role of poetry.

This is no longer true for us, and that is one of the reasons why poets today are less concerned than they used to be to make themselves intelligible to the reader. Communication is subordinated to their private interests, and they expect the reader to take their poetry as one of his private interests also. Of course, not all are like this, but many are. Poetry as an art has come to be more sophisticated than it ever was, and therefore there is doubly a question why it should be considered important.

What counts for much is a fetishism of the creative absolute. Creation is doubtless the most wonderful thing in human experience; to see something come to life is to live in the world of the apparently miraculous. I know nothing more awe-inspiring than to watch in a microscope an egg begin its cleavage and continue its unfolding. The miracle of pseudo-creation is the stock in trade of the fakir and the magician. Art is the symbol of creativeness, detached from utility, existing in its essentiality. The work of art is the ideally complete. Stuffed birds and beasts are gathered into museums; industrial museums gather utensils, textiles, machines. But these are all the same things under conditions other than their natural states. That is not the case with works of art. Each one of them is just itself—something absolute, total, complete, final. They are treasured, almost worshiped, by those who are really quite indifferent to them. The very idea of them is important. No one thinks of the purpose they may have served for religion or national pride; they are just works of art standing for themselves, demanding attention because they are just that which they are.

What is true of art is true of poetry. People buy volumes of poetry, anthologies and collected works, in quantities out of all proportion to what they read. Carlyle said he never bought a book that he did not read from cover to cover, but most people are not like that. Even prose writers, when they are "classics," share in this adoration. "Classics" one might almost define entirely in reference to their authors' names. The difference in price between a picture that is anonymous and the same picture when some authority has given it an honored parent is enormous.

The *Venus* of Giorgione illustrates this, for it was long neglected as a copy by Sassoferrato after Titian, and came to reputation only when Morelli proved it to be a Giorgione. The Great Books are not in the minds of the public what Emerson said they were: things produced in libraries by young men, considered for the most part as rather impudent young men by their respectable contemporaries. To most people philosophers are wise old men, and scientists also, though in fact the production of anything important in the field of thought by elderly persons is rare. Ostwald, the famous chemist, considered compulsory military training the grave of genius, because its routine killed what was budding in the adolescent mind. The sons and daughters of revolutionaries are notoriously conservative, and often it is so with the old age of the adventurous soul "that broke into the silent seas beyond the farthest Hebrides." What he did in youth has become a vested interest.

The papers often speak of the great loss sustained by the country at the death of an old man who, fifty years before, had done something interesting. They do not realize what Stefan Zweig calls to our attention—that while the work remains young, the creator of it grows old. There is one thing more than another worthy of reverence, and that is the creative spirit. But it is better when this is reverenced without fetishism and without auras. The creative spirit is the only source of what is freshly important, but it can miscarry and produce monsters as well as shapely things. Even it is not an absolute good, as cancers painfully prove.

Nor is interest in a work of art always of the re-creative kind. There is an important difference between the appreciation and the estimation of art. A doctor diagnoses a patient impartially, because it is his purpose to do something for the man. So a professional critic attempts to deal with literature and art in order to give the public a kind of prescription, telling them what is good for them. He has a word to say on everything, however great or little may be his real appreciations. In principle he is a kind of judge. The individual reader is not concerned with anything so impersonal. Not every patient absorbs all the drugs the doctor prescribes. So, in matters of appreciation also, man has his idiosyncrasies, his limited capacities, his allergies, his needs. Sometimes advice may help him to profit by his opportunities, but he must be the eventual judge.

One does not always know what one is really in want of. There was a man painting in Paris years ago, an industrious student who was getting nowhere. I told him there were three men he should especially study in the museums: Rubens, Delacroix and Renoir. Like so many earnest students in those days, he thought time spent in the museums was time wasted. He answered that he loathed Rubens—

he was something of a puritan—that he couldn't bear Delacroix, and that he thought Renoir trivial. Anyway, I said, they were what he needed and he had better overcome his aversions sufficiently to look at them more closely. He did, and during his remaining stay in Paris he copied pictures by all three of these men. Later I saw works of his which were definitely in the tradition of Renoir.

One cannot always give such advice with certainty. In this case it was clear to me what he was trying to do, though it was not clear to him. But every case is as particular as are cases for psychoanalysis. This man was capable of certain appreciations, but didn't know what; so he tried to follow what he thought he ought to follow, and do what he was quite incapable of doing. "Clear your mind of cant," said Doctor Johnson; and the cant of unreal appreciations is the special cant of art.

Appreciations are growths, and subject to variation. When I was fifteen I read, while in the country, Tennyson's *Idylls of the King*. I was intensely interested and found one idyll missing; that is, there seemed to be a gap at one place. When I got back to town I happened on a later edition of the poems, and there found what was missing. Tennyson had written a final idyll that fitted in this place. Before that and since, I have read in the *Idylls,* but never since then have I read them with enough interest to notice whether or not the narrative was complete.

When Neilson, later president of Smith College, was a graduate student at Harvard I once noticed in his room a small bookcase full of books by and about Tennyson. I said, "You're greatly interested in Tennyson."

"That sounds as though you're not," he answered.

"No. He reminds me too much of the title of one of his early poems."

"You mean *Thoughts of a Second-rate Sensitive Mind,*" Neilson said.

"Just so."

At fifteen I didn't know that Tennyson's thought was second-rate, but I knew that he could write beautiful verse. Since then, I have ceased to be annoyed by his ideas, and can enjoy without reserve his luminous and perfectly articulated lyrics and his occasional masterpieces of blank verse.

In '94 I was returning from Los Angeles to the East. I had only one book with me, Milton's poems. In the afternoon I began reading *Paradise Lost* and read on with intense interest. I read in my seat till the porter made up the berths. Then I read in the smoking room till the porter made up his berth there. Now there was only one light left, a tiny gaslight at the angle leading to the platform, and I sat under this light on the little bench made for climbing into the upper berths, till Adam and his consort through Eden took their solitary way. Never before or since have I read *Paradise Lost* with such immoderate absorption.

There seems often to be a fatality in these happenings. One picks up a book as though by pure chance, a book that one has read before or that one knows of, and finds it to be just what one wants and needs. Quite unaware that one is choosing, one chooses. A fatal moment has come: there is a need, actual though not consciously felt, and one seizes on the one thing that will satisfy this. This happens, of course, to a growing mind, when fate is still knocking at the door, when all one's possibilities are not yet exhausted—and this, if one is fortunate, will last till the end.

What is true of poetry is likewise true of ideas. This is natural, because philosophy is just poetry that tries to pull itself up higher with logical bootstraps. When one has such illuminating moments, one is (especially when young) convinced that one has something that everyone should appreciate. I recall how at college I heard William James say that all classification is teleological. This seemed to me one of the most important things I had ever heard, and I talked to everyone I knew about classification being teleological. This is basic for pragmatism, which appeared above the horizon only much later. But no one of my acquaintance cared in the least whether classification was teleological or not, or could see any importance in it.

Marsden Hartley, when he was in Paris in '26 or '27, wrote to Stieglitz that I was growing flabby, and amusing myself with an insignificant painter named Coubine. Then Hartley went to Aix-en-Provence, the town of Cézanne, and while there discovered "space." Poussin understood "space," but very few painters since have done so. When Hartley returned to Paris, he again happened on some pictures by Coubine, and spent much time at a gallery where they were to be seen. Coubine is one of the rare masters of space. Space is my especial interest. Hartley had suddenly awakened to something to which he had not before been alive, and saw things differently.

What you don't know won't hurt you, says the proverb. But it often makes you talk nonsense, and what one man sees and another does not, makes intercourse difficult when it has to do with the kinds of things that are not really capable of explanation. The qualities of art are perceived, as it were, by a multitude of senses, and he who hasn't them operative, is not in communication with him who has. The difference between these psychic senses and the physical ones is that the former are not simple but composed, and the compositions are very variable. So it happens that a little juggling and shocking can produce a capacity for seeing, even when rational explanation cannot.

A chapter on reading poetry and seeing pictures must deal with this essential question of *seeing,* for that is the heart of the matter. People commonly assume that they can see, and need only learn what they should look at. My experience contradicts this, and insists on the all-importance of learning to see. The *what* will take care of itself if the *how* has been acquired. I don't mean to say that then one will see everything, as the authorities say you should. But if you remember that the authorities are for the most part commonplace persons who, with no extraordinary qualifications, make criticism their business, there is no reason why you should *so* see things. If you learn to *see,* you will be able to see for yourself, and will be content to skip much of what is offered but does not really concern you. I shall now tell how I went about the business of learning to see.

I was interested in esthetics even in childhood, though I did not know it by that name. When we were children, we used often to go for picnics to Dimond's Canon, which was a few miles from our home in East Oakland. Scrub oak was a common tree in those hills, but I was again and again struck by a little bunch of these that stood at the turning of a road and seemed singularly beautiful. The trees themselves were not exceptional, and it was only after a time that I understood this to be a matter of composition, their somewhat unusual placement at this spot.

Once aware of composition, I noticed it elsewhere and often. When I was fourteen, my brother, who had been at college in the East, brought home some etchings—among them one of apple trees. There were plenty of apple trees all about, and to see why this etching pleased me so I took it into the orchard and compared it with the trees. Then I saw that the artist had simplified and made more evident certain characteristics of the trees themselves—once more a matter of composition—and I improvised a definition of art: that it is nature seen in the light of its significance. Then, recognizing that this significance was one of forms, I added "formal" to "significance." Significant Form was then born for me.

Gradually I came on to realize that art and composition are one. Not that in poetry and painting there is nothing else. Shakespeare goes beyond Milton as much in intellect, in varied knowledge, in penetration, as he does in power of composition. He was great enough to be an immoralist, and to make and sympathize with such a rascal as Falstaff. But insight into human nature and ability to appreciate are not a speciality to artists. They are shared by men and women of the world—politicians, detectives, executives—many of whom see much more deeply and wisely than artists in general do. But they are not artists, and when they give some sort of form to their appreciations, that form is not essential. They do not compose what they have to say in any significant manner, and do not make literature.

Long ago, forty-five years ago, I tried to get to the

bottom of this matter. Up to then I had taken composition as I found it. I had discovered in myself no aptitude for any of the arts, and thought of myself as essentially a scientist—one who tried to find out why and how things were, rather than to create or re-create them. But one day it occurred to me to ask the definite question: how does a painter see when he paints? What he produces is a translation into another medium. The thing seen exists outside, and yet it is presumably not what everyone sees. There must be a possibility of seeing things in such a way that they are related to the picture without being it. The problem was to see, and then to learn what was particular about this way of seeing. There is no use speculating when one can experiment; so I began to experiment.

I put on the table a plate of the kind common in Italy, an earthenware plate with a simple pattern in color, and this I looked at every day for minutes or for hours. I had in mind to see it as a picture, and waited for it to become one. In time it did. The change came suddenly when the plate as an inventorial object, one made up of parts that could be separately listed, a certain shape, certain colors applied to it, and so on, went over into a composition to which all these elements were merely contributory. The painted composition on the plate ceased to be *on* it but became a part of a larger composition which was the plate as a whole. I had made a beginning to seeing pictorially.

What had been begun was carried out in all directions. I wanted to be able to see anything *as* a composition, and found that it was possible to do this. I tried it on everything from a scrap of paper torn from the corner of a sheet, to a line of trees extending half a mile into the distance; and I found that with practice seeing pictures was possible everywhere. I soon found that things could be seen in two ways, pictorially and sculpturally, as though one saw with reference to a plane in front of the object, or with reference to a plane behind the object. In one case the thing was seen as flat, but in deep space, which is the paradox of pictorial composition. In the other, it was seen as round, but in shallow space.

This habit of mine of seeing pictorial composition in nature, of seeing it anywhere and whenever I am so inclined, in little or on the grandest scale, makes me difficult in the acceptance of pictures. Such landscape as Claude's and Turner's is for me picturesque only, not really pictorial. It is landscape as anyone sees it, composed, that is, within the limits of a naturalistic vision. In many cases Cézanne does not get beyond that in his composition as a whole. Only in China and Japan was this higher grade of landscape common, and its greatest master in Europe is Poussin.

The difference between the pictorial and the sculpturesque vision is interesting. In the pictorial one sees as though the pictured thing were seen within the limits of a frame, which marks the plane to which the focus is referred. What lies beyond is in a way brought to this plane, or at least adjusted to it. The recession of planes is rhythmic, and never goes off into a meaningless infinity of distance. The infinities of art are inward and not outward. Every good work of art is a self-contained whole, and that which is not, however many good things it may contain, is fragmentary.

The same is true of the sculptural, though this is applicable only to things rather near. I used often, when sitting opposite persons in a tram, to look at them now as pictures, then as sculpture, simply by changing the focus. The same thing can be done for architecture, and is specially interesting for interiors. In fact, I first noticed this when I saw what a change there was in the space of a corridor beyond an open door. The space grew deep or shallow as I changed the focus from the door to the wall beyond. Further trials led to developments. In the interior of churches with columns, the different effects are striking.

It often happened to me in my earlier experiment that I was not able to complete my nature compositions; and sometimes what might have been, but did not come off, was very beautiful. Then the tension was agonizing; then I used to find myself humming or whistling a certain theme, which would bring the needed relief as though on another plane completion had come. It was always the same theme, which I had not chosen and which I couldn't place. A musical friend with whom I was discussing rhythm, played, for purposes of illustration, what he said was the most intense expression of rhythmic emotion in all music, something from the Ninth Symphony of Beethoven, and that was my theme. I was not aware till then that I remembered anything from the Ninth Symphony, which I had rarely heard. It is many years since I have used it for this purpose, as with practice I came to be able to fill the composition without recourse to any outer aid. But this incident will show how intense may be the demand for total compositional realization.

People have commonly to wait upon the artist to show

them pictures, except when there is something obviously picturesque before them; but if they have become educated to pictorial seeing, this is not at all necessary. The beauty of the world is immensely increased; it becomes all, potentially, beautiful. Every man, woman and child is beautiful, and any group of them. The superabundant beauty becomes at times exasperating; one feels a need of doing something about it; one is almost forced to try being an artist, not only in seeing but in doing; one tries to paint. One soon learns that there is no mystery in the fact that things not beautiful to ordinary vision can be made beautiful in pictures. It is nothing more or less than a question of composition—not, of course, arrangement, which is the ordinary photographer's notion of composition; but the artist's, which I have spoken of at such length.

One is not thrown entirely on his own resources for one's education in composition. It is a commonplace that people learn to see things as they have been habituated to seeing them in the pictures that at any moment are most in view; and so they then seem to people really to be. There was a time when to cultivated people landscape meant Claude Lorraine and his tradition: what did not lend itself to that way of seeing was not pictorially seen at all. Fashions change. For a while Cézanne dominated the vision of many. In any case this thing is a limited affair, and automatic; a great deal more can be done if one has learned the art of creative seeing.

For a long time my favorite landscape in western art (in China where rhythm was religiously infused, landscape painting was something far more profound) was the *Tempest* of Giorgione. Compared with many Claudes, this is a simple affair, but compositionally much farther from a mere arrangement. Many a time I have gone to Venice, when I would not have gone if that picture had not been there. I don't much like Venice, where I feel confined, and annoyed by the ever-recurrent perspectives down the canals. Giorgione came from the mainland, like Titian, and did not paint Venetian landscapes. The *Tempest* was long in private possession and, though easy of access, was not as satisfactorily seen as pictures in a public gallery. At last it was bought by the state and put in the Academy; then I could go to Venice and look at it as long as I liked. Once I spent a whole morning with it and made a pencil sketch of it. Then I had *really* seen it, and it was no longer important to me. The next time I went to Venice I spent a few minutes with it, and found it richly pleasant, but no more.

Just what had happened? Art, as I say and resay, is composition. What goes into composition is sometimes more important than at other times. So I feel in the work of Piero della Francesca or of Michelangelo the expression of an intellectual power which is itself interesting, even though I do not try to find out what it specifically says. There is the difference between a Herrick or Beaumont and Fletcher and a Donne or Shakespeare. T. S. Eliot has admirably expressed this when he says that to Donne "a thought was an experience, it modified his sensibility."

In Donne this is shown nakedly, as though he paused to digest the thought, while Shakespeare takes it in his stride. So with Piero compared with Michelangelo. In Giorgione I feel nothing of this sort. His lyric feeling is essentially song—though at a high level of intelligence, which makes his form splendid and thrilling. But when once fully assimilated, while it has lost none of its charm, it has lost much of its power.

When I had really assimilated this form in its essentials, I no longer needed it. I had taken to painting again at this time, and found that everything I did was composed like the *Tempest* of Giorgione. There was nothing similar in the arrangement; there was nothing similar in the subject matter; there was nothing similar in the mood. I am sure that to no one would it have occurred that there was any relation whatever between what I was doing and the Giorgione, and yet I felt that somehow I was seeing things in his terms. I preferred Hsia Kuei and some other Sung landscape painters, but I couldn't grasp their compositions as I could Giorgione's. It wasn't more difficult to analyze theirs, so far as analysis can go, but I couldn't make them mine. I couldn't arrive at seeing in their terms except when by chance something suggested them.

After a while I outgrew this Giorgione compositional phase, and my work suggested no one else's to me until I happened to see reproductions of earlier Chinese work, landscapes of the Tang period, with which I felt an affinity; but this time it was just an affinity, not an influence.

I am always uncertain when speaking of these things how far a reader can get what I mean. It is simple enough if one has had experience of this kind, but one does not know what the experiences of another are. Certainly most persons who are not artists are too passive in their seeing to be creative seers—though this is not due to incapacity, but to lack of this kind of exercise. In America it seems now to be necessary that all college students should learn something of the significance of an art, should learn to appreciate it. I am convinced by my own experience that a little active practice in seeing goes much farther than a great deal of concern with art that does not involve activity of this sort. Passive receptivity gives something that has little growing power, and one usually stops taking interest before long. To be sure, one may go on with exhibition visiting, but the succession of these events amounts to little more than a panorama, and has small cultural value.

For education in hearing, there is nothing comparable to the practice in composition that the visible world offers. For music and speech, we are thrown back on human efforts. There is the compensation of a wide field of possible interpretation, since music has to be played or sung, and in the reading of poetry one must, if one is to get its full value, read it word for word as though one read it aloud—which is a kind of acting with voice, if not with the body.

A principal education in words is to use them as though they were living things, sensitive to use or to abuse. Once a nephew of eight was to spend the summer with us in Fiesole: one small boy and four grown-ups. To keep him occupied, I suggested he should make a collection of butterflies, but his father objected that the boy was rather callous and should not be set to killing things. So I explained to him that insects did not suffer pain in any sense to which we could give a meaning, but that indiscriminate killing was bad for the killer, even if it was only a wanton knocking off the heads of flowers in crossing a field. Therefore he should catch butterflies for his collection, and no more. This he quite conscientiously did.

Words also do not actually suffer when one misuses them, though it has been said of some poets that their words would bleed if they were cut. But it is certain that the person who uses words indifferently, who uses them as though they were rubber stamps, who never stops to find out what exactly the words he uses or reads mean, is not on the high cultural road. Only the other day I read of some business man who disliked rubber stamps as a means of correspondence, but found himself obliged to return to them, because otherwise he was misunderstood, or not understood at all. People commonly find in books not exactly what the author put in, but what is easy to understand or to suppose that one has understood. Only a few discover what fascinating things words are—how admirably they can be fitted together, like the works of a watch, to say things with delicate discrimination. For the book to be taken to the traditional desert island, few would prove more interesting than an unabridged dictionary, and the ten volumes of the Oxford Dictionary might make one wish that it were possible to retire with it to a deserted, if not quite a desert, island for more than a year or two.

It is not, of course, necessary to define words. Ability to define is a special gift, and not at all common. In some cases it is almost an evil, for many words have so many meanings, meanings central and peripheral, that definitions clog one's perceptions. It is almost as vicious at times as the practice, common when I went to school, of "paraphrasing" poetry—that is, perverting it into prose. Poetry is not something to translate into something else; it is something to be read and reread till it reveals its secrets. It is better to read one poem ten times than to read ten poems once. All that one should do in aid is to find out the meanings of unknown words and the sense of unknown allusions; the rest should come from acquaintance with the text.

Words in poetic and in prosaic utterance have very different values. For prose purposes it is necessary only that one should know what is meant, what is intended, what is referred to. I think that one very good way of distinguishing the prosaic and the poetic is to see that one is referential and the other existential. That is a summary abstract statement which it will be worth developing.

Keats in the *Eve of St. Agnes:*

> *Forth from the close[t] brought a heap*
> *Of candied apple, quince and plum and gourd:*
> *With jellies soother than the creamy curd*
> *And lucent syrups tinct with cinnamon;*
> *Manna and dates in argosy transferred*
> *From Fez, and spiced dainties, every one,*
> *From silken Samarcand to cedar'd Lebanon.*

Compare this to a bill of lading from some eastern merchant in which these articles are itemized. For the merchant, the articles have a real existence, but the words of the invoice have merely a referential value. For the poet, the articles serve merely the purpose of the words.

For the poet these articles might not, if actually present, suggest to him at all what the words, as he has come to understand them, mean. His experience may be like that of the bored people abroad who do not find, when they travel, the objects of their dreams. For the merchant it is quite the contrary. If the things are not really what the words have implied that they are, the shipment will be rejected. For the prosaic we need merely know exactly what the words mean—that is, to what they refer—but for the purpose of the poetic we must also know what meanings are so intimately tied up with the words here and now, that the words carry the things meant with them. Such words are poetic words, many of them commonplaces like roses and nightingales. The splendid poem of Keats from which I quoted is largely made up of poetic words, though not so shopworn. But in the last scene of *Lear,* Shakespeare gets along without poetic words. It is a composition of meanings and sounds expressed in simple words which become existential by being charged with the meaning of the whole.

An excellent illustration is the line from Wordsworth's *Michael* that Matthew Arnold quotes as typically Wordsworthian: "And never lifted up a single stone." One might say of a lazy workman, "He's been out there, just loafing, for an hour and never lifted up a single stone," and no one would think this great poetry; most would not even recognize that there are two perfectly good iambic pentameters. These lines would have no existential value; they would simply call attention to the lazy workman. But the compositional use by Wordsworth of his line makes it something entirely different. These simple words become weighted with the tragedy of the old shepherd, and are saturated with poetry. Their referential importance is slight, for the importance of the action to which they refer is not in the action itself, but in the meaning; and that meaning is borne by the words. Therefore this is a line of great poetry.

"Existential" and "inferential" point the mind toward

"illustration." Illustration has an ordinary meaning—simply to illustrate—but it has also a pejorative meaning, when we say of a picture that it is "mere illustration." This means that the interest of the picture is not self-contained, but refers away from itself to an object outside. In the first sense, almost all the world's great painting is illustration; but in the second sense it is not. When the good dramatic painters paint a dramatic episode, the drama is complete in itself. This does not mean that the subject must of necessity not count. In Shakespeare it makes no difference whether we have ever before heard of Macbeth or Lear; they are in all senses fully contained in the play. But this is not true of Julius Caesar or Antony and Cleopatra. Here we are expected to know more about the characters and the period than is told in the plays. But that knowledge we bring to the play; we are not sent out to it.

To be sent out to it is the characteristic of illustration—of the usual historical narrative, for instance. It may also be the characteristic of a philosophical style. In an article I once wrote, I pointed out that it was practicable to read William James in the text itself, but that to understand Dewey, one had better keep one's attention fixed more on what he was talking about than on the text itself. Dewey's writing is not creative, whatever his thought may be. James wrote existentially and Dewey referentially.

In Walt Whitman there is much to the point when we think about illustration. Sometimes he succeeds in realizing the objects that he names, but often these names are mere names that bring to mind the objects which have then to be made real by the imagination of the reader. In this there is poetic expression at second hand. One is referred to the object which excites a poetic interest which was not adequately realized in the first statement.

Great writers in their successful moments realize at first hand, and then their expression is commonly of extreme precision. For prosaic purposes this precision is limited to meanings—to reference. It serves essentially the purpose of construction. To repeat in this context what has already been said, engineering is construction and architecture is composition. Scales are construction and melody is composition. Imitative painting or modeling is construction and art is composition. Prosaic writing is construction and poetic writing is composition. Just as for architecture there must be a basic construction, so for all the other arts. But for the prosaic, in all forms of expression the constructive is sufficient. For the poetic it is never sufficient; the compositional from which the existential derives is essential.

Most works that are important for their poetic value have incidental prose values. Incidental values are, of course, legitimate. One can use precious brocades to keep oneself warm or even to wipe up the floor, but this is not making the best use of them. When Dante and Milton argue, they are often both dull and unconvincing. Poets are rarely great or original thinkers, and even if they were, their medium is not adapted to the adequate expression of critical thought except in epigram. It is difficult enough to express subtle thinking referentially without being obliged to find for it an adequate existential form. But since only few people are interested in exact thinking, what they get out of the poets may be good enough for them. It is not, however, the best that poetry has to give. Its best is appreciations, for which existential expression, through the power of composition, is especially adapted.

Words are marvelous materials for construction and composition, but one must make them adaptable by constantly using them as a good mechanic uses his tools. Everybody recognizes that careless use of the instrument will not give satisfactory results, but they do not see that they cannot be really intelligent about anything being discussed until they learn to use the tools which are necessary—that is, the meaning of words, and the putting them together into sentences and discourses. There is a fascination in watching a real master of language fit meaning to purpose with the exquisite precision of a jeweler. "Your reasons at dinner have been sharp and sententious: pleasant without scurrility, witty without affectation, audacious without impudency, learned without opinion, and strange without heresy."

Thus Shakespeare, every word clean-cut and telling. One can write like that only if one loves words. Or this of Johnson, on Dryden: "Of him that knows much it is natural to believe that he has read with diligence, yet I rather believe that the knowledge of Dryden was gleaned from accidental intelligence and various conversation, by a quick apprehension, a judicious selection, and a happy memory, a keen appetite of knowledge, and a powerful digestion, by vigilance that permitted nothing to pass notice, and a habit of reflection that suffered nothing useful to be lost." Only the habit of precision in the use of words makes it possible to have such exquisite discrimination in ideas.

For science, words are often not accurate enough, and

instead, symbols and equations are used. But the paradox of words in poetry is their combination of precision and imprecision. The cheap poet can easily get his effect by using words that pour over their natural confines of meaning—loves and doves, roses and woeses, home and mother, Alabama and Dolores. None the less, dozens of good poems in all languages have been written on so hackneyed a subject as the advice that you had better have a good time while you can—with girls and roses to illustrate. Here it is as in music: a subtle difference in composition, and there is something vitally different, even new. For the bad poet, the words slip into place as though they were greased; for the good poet, they go into place as though they were jeweled. Nor is it necessary, in order to be bad, that the words should be of the sappy poetic kind. Today, especially in poetry of the proletarian sort, one finds quantities written in the plainest language, which is as flat as a city square, the words as little distinguished by their placements as the pavement blocks. These words do not bleed if you cut them, any more than do those blocks.

All that is here said of words is true of forms. A few years ago, the walls of exhibitions were covered with Cézannesque still-lifes which were quite without rhyme or reason. They made me think of the sword combat between Tom Sawyer and Joe Harper: "When you get the hang of it go it lively."

That is a show that repeats itself in all fields. If you are doing the latest thing, you can feel at least a little bit important. I recall the disgust of a young fellow in Paris when I said that I was a pragmatist at a time when everybody who was up to snuff was a phenomenologist. You had to be impressed by the *neue Sachlichkeit,* even if that was all the German you knew—just as a few years before, you were all agog over the *élan vitale.*

Now it is Kierkegaard who has the cry. When Kierkegaard wrote, he was really important; but today, after pragmatism, Freud and a lot of other things, he is resurrected because now anyone can understand him. As literature he remains; as revelation he reveals as in a glass darkly, what has been much more clearly stated. Like Vico a few years ago, he becomes a contemporary prophet, for the contemporary prophet is often a resurrection. People love to say, "I told you so," and they get much satisfaction in telling the discoverers of their own time that these things have already been discovered.

Probably there will be a crop of little Kierkegaards as there was a crop of little Nietzsches. There are many people really uncreative, who can get the illusion of creation if they are a few feet ahead of the masses, no matter how far they are behind the leaders. What they write has either the flatness or the frothiness of the second-rate. Their variations on the original theme are hardly more than lipstick and rouge. Their changes of the original constructions make these a little more shaky, and their compositions are too artificial to permit a life-blood of rhythm to flow through them.

One cannot too much insist that the vitality of appreciation is re-creation. Of course being rocked in the cradle of the deep is a great delight, but it is a passing thing. Lorelei told the truth when she said that kissing one's hand is very nice, but a diamond bracelet lasts for ever.

William James made an oft-quoted, though usually misquoted, remark: that those who were not really musical should work off their emotion by doing something active, even if it were only speaking a kind word to their aunt. The quoters usually ignore the essential distinction between the musical, who can re-create, and the unmusical, who cannot.

Saying a kind word to one's aunt is re-creation on another plane. When one can get into a sort of tit-for-tat relation to art (you make me, I make you); when you can feel that the artist has started something which you are completing on his terms and on yours, until (as I have illustrated with the Giorgione landscape) the original work remains in essence a stage in your journey and a delightful memory, while you go on to further possibilities—then you are getting the esthetic experience in its essential richness, something which cannot be summed up as an emotional debauch, but is an experience which is rich in all the qualities proper to the intellect and the imagination.

One can hardly discuss hearing and seeing without going on to criticism, a very complicated subject. *Criticism makes, explains and justifies discriminations.* When Sam Weller was puzzled by a blotted word in his valentine, a word beginning with "circum," his father—to whom the valentine was being read—suggested "circumwented," but finally Sam made it out to be "circumscribed." The father thought "circumwented" was a better word, but Sam thought "circumscribed" meant more; and his father agreed that perhaps it was a "more tenderer" word.

These are, of course, very delicate discriminations, which only sophisticated connoisseurs like Sam and Tony Weller could make, but ordinary critics have to deal with similar matters. Words in poetry often make trouble for one. There are not only individual but also epochal differences. We can read Donne, but the eighteenth century could not. His wide popularity is quite recent. In '95 I tried to find a Donne, but there was none in print. The following year, the *Muses Library* was made to include him, and now he is abundant. The romantics of the nineteenth century found the diction of the eighteenth atrocious, but they could not realize that the eighteenth century would have found it atrocious also if it had sounded to them as it did to the romantics. That is one of the difficulties of criticism. The critic makes the extravagant assumption that he is normal, and can therefore serve as a standard.

Today, in consequence of modern psychology, more people are aware that they are peculiar, but their awareness does not change them. Bertrand Russell, in an essay criticizing John Dewey, says that he recognizes his own peculiarities, and that these will affect his criticism; therefore he will begin by a statement of these peculiarities. But once the statement is made, the peculiarities are ignored. Really, they ought to be factors in the ultimate equation, but they are not. Reaction times are, when necessary, accounted for in accurate experiments or observations—astronomical ones, for instance. But criticism is, in any case, not an exact science; so these idiosyncrasies are not necessarily a disadvantage. Critics are useful for a variety of purposes, but delivering a final judgment is not one of them. A principal role they play is to discover things and bring them to the attention of others, and often their eccentricities make them particularly sensitive to new and valued expressions.

Works of art have to be discovered by someone who will make known what he has found, for only the few can do this work for themselves. Of course, discovery is not an absolute affair, except in rare cases. Norman Douglas told me he once heard a servant at a hotel singing something that he recognized as Wagnerian, though it was unknown. The servant, he found on enquiry, had worked for Wagner, in Venice I think, and had heard Wagner sing this. So Douglas wrote it out, and added to the stock of Wagnerian music. In most cases, someone discovers something for a certain public, although others may already know this. When Stanley said, "Dr. Livingstone, I presume," he was discovering Livingstone for Europeans, though the Negroes in Africa already knew where he was. Discovering and rediscovering goes on indefinitely. Things are forgotten. Critics discover aspects that were ignored. Critics discover things that they didn't know before, and think that no one else did. Discovering things is great fun, and therefore critics never tire of the game.

Works of art have many dimensions, and the critic can help to bring these to light and emphasize their value. Of course I do not here refer to dimensions of space; I am speaking of qualitative and not spatial dimensions. Everyone knows that sex makes a difference in art, that a portrait of a woman brings a higher price than the portrait of a man, without regard to difference in merit. Sex has a specific value of interest incommensurable with any other quality, and for that reason I call it a dimension. This dimension needs no critic for its revelation, but it is not so with others. A picture by a known painter does not look exactly like a picture by an unknown painter, even to a person who values it independently of this. What lies in the back of the mind influences what is seen, and the awareness of the author places and warms the object. It gets to have not only an individual but a family interest.

For this reason, critical connoisseurship has its importance, even for appreciation. Then there is historical criticism—not merely as history, for that is another matter, but for reasons analogous to authorship. Just as our consciousness of a man's descent or race colors our sense of the man, so it is with works of art. It does not make them better or worse, but makes them different; and so I call this another dimension. One can think of others: subject matter, types of landscape, propaganda. The conservative has his dimension, the radical another, and so the bourgeois or the proletarian.

I have just been reading a book of proletarian writing. I was much interested, and as I believe that socialism is the only possible solution for the society of the future—though I have no program for making it work—I was much in sympathy with it. Yet I know that I cannot possibly realize it as can those whose experience it approximates. There are dimensions of social understanding which are different for them and me. I may point out in such a work some formal insufficiency which another may agree to, and yet we may disagree entirely concerning the effect of this on the whole work. Therefore criticism is a relative thing.

I know only one value character of the work of art where there seems possible an objective decision. In a considerable experience of art criticism, and a very little one of literary criticism, it has seemed to me that one can give a definite answer as to whether a certain formal result has been completely realized. When I am asked for an opinion on his work by a painter, I never criticize anything but this. Of other things I just talk as anyone does if something has to be said, but I don't take that kind of talk seriously. But about formal completion I mean business.

A formally complete picture is one in which all the parts are so related to one another that they all imply each other. If one looks at one spot in a picture and does not have one's eye pulled to other spots, and so on over the whole picture till every bit of it is implicated in the operation, the picture is incomplete. This is the meaning of the oft-repeated story of Cézanne and the two uncovered spots in a portrait. Why did he leave those spots uncovered? Because he did not know just what ought to go there, and the wrong thing would falsify the whole.

Perhaps no one except Cézanne would have noted this; perhaps they would. I don't know. Once Matisse was working on a picture that measured over eight by twelve feet. It was hung high on a wall, in a position like that which it was to have in a palace in Moscow. Matisse and I were sitting below, talking, while his mind ran partly on the picture. Several times he mounted the ladder and slashed at the picture with big brushes, making big changes in it. Once, after a long pause and some silent meditation, he climbed the ladder and altered a line on the neck of one figure, flattening just a little bit a line a couple of inches long. When he came down, I said, "I've understood everything you did before this last change, but I don't see the point of that."

He replied, "I'm not surprised, because I've decided to change entirely the orientation of the figures." Perhaps if

Cézanne had put the wrong color on those bare places that too would have been obvious.

I have noticed over and over again that if one points out to a painter that there is a hole in his picture, he agrees. Often he says that he too has noticed it, but did not know what he should put there. Once a painter said to me, "It's damnable, but every time there is a spot in my picture where I didn't know what to put, and put something as a makeshift, you light on it."

Composition is my passion. I have already told how I cultivated it, and the intense demand there was in me for the completion of composition. Often when the painter cannot find the last word, I can find it for him. The best painters find it for themselves, but the lesser ones often stop short; their creative energy does not carry through. A French painter whom I knew slightly asked me to look at his work. He showed me a lot of pictures, but almost all incomplete. As I did not know how he would take it, I made conventional remarks, but at last could not help pointing to a hole and suggesting how it could be filled. He was pleased, and asked whether I had noticed anything else. I said I had noticed many things; so we went all over the pictures again, and he learned a lot about composition.

To fill a hole in a picture does not usually mean that something should be put into that place. It usually means that the relations existing are inadequate. Once I pointed to such a hole in a picture of an interior.

"Yes," said the painter. "I noticed that and thought I'd put a chair in there."

"That is not what is needed. You don't want to clutter up your picture with objects. If the relations between this and that were right, there wouldn't be any hole." And so it was.

I could give dozens of instances, some of them amusing; but as this sounds too much like bragging, I shall pass them over. But in fact what interests me in these instances is not the element of "I" but the element of "it," the fact that this is the kind of thing in art on which consensus is possible. It is extraordinary to a person who never had the experience before, when he is shown how in a picture a slight change often remote from the point where the trouble is, where the hole is, fills that up completely and alters entirely the pictorial totality. An eighth or even a sixteenth of an inch on quite a large canvas may do the trick, or an almost imperceptible spot of color. It is a satisfaction to know that in painting there is something of which it can be said that it is right or wrong.

The works of the old painters were almost never complete in this sense. When one speaks of triangular composition or rather pyramidal, of oval composition or S-shaped and so on, one generally refers to the figures or the principal objects. In completeness a picture in a rectangular frame cannot be anything but a rectangular composition. But the older painters were primarily illustrators: they were working for a public that wanted pictures of things, saints, scenes from Holy Script, drama, *genre,* still life. Consequently there was a distinction between the subject and the accessories. A Giorgione or a Rubens went beyond this, but it must have been a product of their personal genius, for they don't seem to have taught it to their followers. But even if the pictures had been more unified as compositions than they were, that unity would long since have been destroyed by darkening and repaint, or have been converted into a sort of unity of tone.

I once made the effort to look at pictures in the Louvre exactly as I look at pictures of today, but I found it a great strain. There was a marked resistance to breaking up the familiar things, as was inevitable when one ceased to make the automatic allowance for the discolorations, the false values, the disappearance of essential contours in the murk of obscurity. One must in great measure take the old masters as one takes Greek sculpture—as more or less fragmentary, and often restored to the point of being hardly more than copies. Fortunately, where the basis is substantial much is left, even in the ruins. Matisse once pointed to the difference in two plaster casts that I had of heads by Donatello and Michelangelo. In the Donatello, he said, if one cut away the surface modeling nothing would be left, but the Michelangelo could be rolled down a hill till most of the surface elements were knocked off, and the form would still remain. So it is with the greatest of the older painters, though many of the pictures in the museums are of little value, except as specimens.

Criticism, I have said, makes, explains and justifies discriminations. Many people have little interest in criticism. They simply accept things or reject them, and are the little ones of whom is the kingdom of heavenly innocence. But others are more cantankerous. They roundly assert that what they like is good and what they don't like is bad. When you ask them why, they say that they don't know why; it isn't a matter for reasoning; anyone can see that this is good and that isn't. These are people who make discriminations, but don't explain or justify them.

Then there are those who explain. They have knowledge, much or little of technique in verse or paint; they have ideas about form and matter, origins and development; and they are often instructive, but rarely amusing. They can tell much about a work of art, but not what it finally is—why it is definitely successful, or a failure. This depends on differences like those between a copy and an original, differences that may be obvious or so subtle that only the extra-sensitive can perceive them. This shows the limit of explanation of masterpieces.

Next comes the justification of discrimination, and here things become really exciting and the fur starts to fly. Here come to words, and sometimes to fisticuffs, the differences between the ancients and the moderns, classic and romantic, moralists and immoralists, abstract and concrete, academic and freethought, bourgeois and proletarian, and many others. Man was not born to full protection, and one thing he commonly needs to keep him warm is opinions. Without opinions he feels unarmed, even naked. I have just read in the papers of someone who had been a communist, but because communism aims at a tyranny of the human spirit, he left communism and joined the Catholic church—which, as everyone knows, welcomes the rebels and the independents. He is to teach in a Catholic college, and will doubtless be free to teach whatever he likes. Evidently this is a man who cannot stand freezing in the winter cold of uncertainty. If he next becomes a freethinker, he will certainly feel free to do everything except think freely, and will tie up to an authoritative freethinker, so as to feel safe.

Most people are like that. They naturally join something

and are then on the defensive or the aggressive, according to differences of character. I once, while living in Paris, subscribed for six months to a communist and to a clerical newspaper, but long before the six months were over I had stopped reading both—they were so impossibly stupid. One knew what they would say about everything, and that they were as much interested in the truth as members of a Piscatorial Club. Of course the more able members of the different groups and directions often say admirable things, while justifying their opinions. They mingle explanation and justification artfully and sometimes luminously—T. S. Eliot, for instance.

Criticism of art does not confine itself to formal or quasi-formal matters. There is in some poets, and in a few painters, an intellectual content of so much importance that it becomes seriously interesting. Though they do not, like philosophers, make systems which are attempted constructions, they do make what one might call compositions of thought which are impressive. Poets like Shakespeare, Dante, Goethe, Wordsworth, Leopardi, men of mind, contrast with Herrick, Lovelace, Elizabethan lyricists, poets who sing beautifully, but say little that is not obvious. Between them are men like Herbert, Crashaw, Gray, Tennyson, Byron, who say things that they feel to be important, but whose importance is not first-rate.

In those greatest men one realizes their ethical, religious or social significance, without the need of any formulation. These are expressed in the values of a compositional object, the values of living things presented as plastic realities. This sort of thing marks the unique quality of *Don Quixote,* of *Hamlet,* of Milton's *Satan,* of *Achilles* and

Odysseus, of Blake, of Donne, of Goethe's *Faust*. If one forgets the Elizabethan lyrics one has left over only an aroma of sweetness, but if one has really known Wordsworth and can't recall a single line, Wordsworth will remain. Criticism of these characteristics is, however, not often criticism of poetry. The compositional values must be taken massively and directly, and the critical discussion of these things too often becomes ethical and philosophical.

In pictures there is something analogous to these qualities in literature. In Michelangelo, there is the supreme power of a really great creative mind. He makes on me a curiously contradictory impression, to which I know no parallel—that of a destructive, crushing force engaged in creation, a cross between Genesis and the Day of Judgment. It was a coincidence that he painted the Last Judgment on the wall of the Sistine Chapel after having illustrated Genesis on the ceiling—a coincidence, for he did both because commissioned thereto. But it seems like a fatality, like just what he ought to have done to fulfill his destiny, and he did them in such a manner as to make every other treatment since then seem a slight affair.

Many other painters have merits of this sort. Piero della Francesca seems like a monumental veracity, like something indefeasibly authentic. Cézanne is similar, though on a lower intellectual level. A suggestion of intellectual vigor almost always goes with these cases. Even in Giorgione, perhaps the greatest of all lyric painters, I feel that only an intellectual grasp could have given that massive richness which makes his *Sleeping Venus* unique among nudes. In Renoir I feel this less. He seems to me to be the man who lifted the picturesque to the highest level of the pictorial, but whose feeling was none the less essentially of the picturesque. Of course this kind of criticism is sketchy and impressionistic, but most analytic criticism is nothing but a lumbering effort to expand such impressions. No real analysis of the essential is possible, because one has to deal with imponderables. But it is fun to try to put in words these indeterminate apprehensions; some readers will understand them, and some will not.

Criticism serves intrinsic appreciation of art only as an introduction. When I was young I liked to read critical works, but now I can read very few of them. One reason is that it is almost all familiar, for the range of critical ideas is not great. Another thing is that my facility of contact with the works themselves continually augments, my sense of them grows more keen, my capacity to take what I want and leave what I don't, develops; and so I need no intermediates. Criticism of what I do not see or read is uninteresting because I don't know what is being talked about, and what I can get at I prefer to know by the only effective way—by repeated contact. It is better to read a difficult poem a dozen times, than to read it once and then have it explained to you. In the one case the process of re-creation takes place and in the other it does not. To get to know what a poem is about is not a matter of importance. Other kinds of books are more important, if one wants to know what things are about. It is best to take poetry for its poetic value, if one can. Of course, if one cannot, one must do what is possible.

There are one or two more things that must be treated while we are on criticism—what is meant by bad art, and what is meant by good?—what is beautiful, and what is ugly? Good art is that which is better than the average of what one is familiar with, and bad art is that which is worse. Therefore with experience one's standard rises.

Every other definition I know is arbitrary. If I call Van Gogh's painting bad, and someone else calls it good, it is because it falls below my standard in qualities which I consider essential, and it does not do so for the other man. It may be possible for me to make the other man understand what are my standards, or it may not—that depends on a lot of things—but the fact that Van Gogh is now held at so high a rate is for my appreciations a matter of no importance. I have tested him, and find that he doesn't stand it. I agree with his own opinion that he had barely reached the end of his apprenticeship, and it is possible that if he had preserved his sanity and gone on painting, he might have arrived. Those who find that he had arrived have not the same demands determined by their experience of art as I have, and so we must amiably agree to differ.

It is, of course, not difficult to understand the enthusiasm for Van Gogh. He was essentially a popular painter, who missed popularity because the populace of his time was not ready to see as pictures what was not "finished." His violent, unrestrained temper, his passionate sympathies, his coarse intense colors hurled at the canvas, often in masses so as to produce impetuous effects, all serve the moment. There is on the one hand today much so-called primitivism, and on the other an amount of pseudo-intellectuality that is absolutely laughable. I have just been looking over a lot of American art magazines of the war, and find even the purpose of special exhibitions defined in intellectual terms. Painters who never would have guessed that they had intellects if this news hadn't been forced on them, now intellectualize. There is an orgy of pitiable intellectuality. So between popular vision and intellectual interpretations, Van Gogh has a wonderful time.

Now comes the turn to say something of the beautiful, of that which is not the beautiful, and of the ugly. The beautiful has not so far been mentioned in this book. I dislike the word, as used in any other than a popular sense, because so much that is pretentiously meaningless, vaguely pretentious, highfalutin', has been talked about it from the time of Plato on, and I don't suppose that Plato was the one who began it. Simply, the beautiful means the attractive, the agreeable, the ordered, the pleasing, the charming, the gracious, even the comfortable. It runs the scale from the trivially pleasant to the cosmically passionate and the ideally complete. There are no frontiers between its widely ranging degrees. The opposite to the beautiful is not the ugly, but the opposites to all the things that make up the beautiful. These are the repulsive, the repellent, the discordant, the disordered, the disturbing, irritating, annoying, troubling, awkward, clumsy, gawky. The ugly has a different dimension. It is not a primary notion at all, but is related to choice. Nothing is ugly, except by contrast, except when we think it ought to be something else. It implies a disappointment in expectation, not necessarily a real expectation, but at least an as-if one. We don't really expect a mule or a donkey to be a horse, but if we did not know horses we would have a different feeling about mules and donkeys. In themselves, no things are ugly.

Matisse once used a pretty girl as model for a statuette which turned out to be something queer—a long cylindrical torso, a large-featured, distorted face, long bunchy legs. The girl looked at the finished product and said, "How awfully ugly."

"Yes," said Matisse. "Isn't it?"

The girl looked a while longer. "Of course it's ugly, it's awfully ugly, and yet—and yet, there's something about it—something that isn't exactly ugly."

Matisse was, of course, interested, and tried to get more.

"Well, of course it's ugly, but yet there's something about it—something different, something—oh—oh I don't know what I mean," she ended, half in tears with the irritation.

Of course, once more, what she meant was simple enough. When she first looked at the figure, she thought of it as the portrait of the pretty girl who had posed. So considered, it was ugly, and no question. But as she looked longer, she began to see qualities that were intrinsic, and these were, in part at least, not ugly. It was ugly when regarded in terms of expectation, but it was beautiful, somehow, when taken by itself. Not altogether beautiful, because it still remained in some ways unattractive, even repulsive—but somehow beautiful.

What is true of Matisse's statuette is true of all cases of the ugly, as distinguished from the unbeautiful. A girl who is not ugly at all when selling apples in the market, is ugly as a chorus girl. She is out of place. The chorus as a whole may be made unbeautiful, that is, disordered by the presence of such ugly girls. But it would become ugly only if considered as out of place in the larger setting of the whole scene. What is unbeautiful may be ugly, but it need not so be. Often the unbeautiful, even the repulsive, is not at all ugly, because it is taken as right in the existing relations, as for instance the unpleasant subjects of many Velasquez portraits. Only those would consider them there as ugly, who think that all people in pictures should be in themselves attractive. Matisse's girl was simple enough to follow the lead of her impression, and to see what one could hardly have expected her to see. Matisse himself did not expect it. Many so-called cultured people cannot make this passage, because they think they "know."

It is natural that in art, as well as in nature, much that is indifferent or even beautiful should at first acquaintance be held as ugly. This is commonly true of unfamiliar works, of other races, unusual landscapes, eccentric vegetable growths. Like Matisse's girl, we first think in terms of the expected, and as these are disappointed, our appreciations are frustrated. Only the experienced in these matters are willing to wait, to see what will be revealed. Matisse's girl, if she were a very unusual person, would on the next occasion be more cautious in judgment, but if she were like most people it would take many such experiences to produce an effect. Until the present moment, when it is common to throw up one's hands and cry "Kamerad," no matter what impossibilities are offered to one's sight, people found ugly whatever was new. Ruskin was as much offended by the "blotesque" of Corot as Kenyon Cox was by the massacres of Matisse, and both had the same justification in the habits and conventions of so-called civilized people. Although these are not so rigid as the habits and conventions of more primitive folks, yet who is to decide how rigid they should be? Kenyon Cox was a conscientious person. He believed that he had fairly looked at the things that he rejected, both because they were unbeautiful—unpleasant or even repellent—and ugly—being the things that they ought not to be. It is not always the person who accepts readily who turns out in the long run to be "right." Here as everywhere, for the subjects discussed in this book, there are no definable limits.

There remains one more question of criticism: contemporary and permanent importance. Permanence is commonly considered to be almost decisive as a value, a final pronouncement on the worth of a work. I take issue with this, and believe permanence to be a minor matter, except for practical reasons. With respect to nature, we all know this. Sunsets and sunrises, June days and storms, are held as valuable as granite cliffs and sequoias. In art it is the same. There are important things that last longer than more important things that come and go. The poetry of Byron is vastly more important, even if little read today, than much that remains current. Every anthology of the past has a proportion of poems that are dropped from the anthologies that succeed it, but they are not necessarily less important for any other characters than the particular ones that insure permanence. There are little songs of the Elizabethans or the Cavalier poets that were slight things when they were made and which are slight things today: that is, they are perfect trifles, and therefore immortal. But to say that they should be held more important than Blair's *Grave* or Young's *Night Thoughts,* which nobody reads, or Thomson's *Seasons,* which few read, is nonsense.

If one wants to make sense of such an assertion, one must limit it. Things can be rendered permanent by the effective importance of what is said or by the fine perfection in the saying. Things that do not sufficiently excel in either way fall sooner or later, but in the meanwhile they may have greatly worked upon the current of events, artistically or socially. Consider Volney's *Ruins, Ossian, Paul and Virginia*. There are many of these things. What is influential has its own kind of importance, and things that are merely pleasant cannot be put into comparison. When things can keep their power of influence endlessly and be also masterpieces of expression, we have the Shakespeares, the Dantes and the Michelangelos, where it is a mockery to put the names in the plural; but for lesser things we must discriminate. For today what counts is what does today's work. It is pleasant to think that it did work also yesterday and the day before, but this is value of a secondary kind. "Antiques" is not only an unbeautiful word, it is also ugly —in my technical sense. It implies that things have merit because they are old. It is best that all things should be put on an equality for testing; an insistence on the value of the old obscures the sense of art as something live.

The classics are, in a general way, the works that last. For any particular age, they are the works of the past that have lasted up to then. For today, they are the works that we still acknowledge; that we gather into museums, select libraries, anthologies; and treasure in reproductions. To be more exact, however, we should recognize that classics, to be a vital term, should be a term expressed in relation to those for whom the classics exist. I wander through museums and see a lot of stuff that could for all of me be thrown into the ash barrel. They are classics for somebody, no doubt—but what isn't? I have come to distinguish between the classics and the "classics." To find out what the classics are, I read them or look at them. To find out what the "classics" are, I look into the books of the authorities. When I agree with the authorities I can wipe out the distinction; when I can't I must insist on it.

For an example: I have repeatedly during the last thirty years or more tried to read *The Wings of the Dove* and *The Golden Bowl* of Henry James. I could appreciate the marvelous style, the mastery over words, the closeness with which he kept those words in contact with his ever-shifting, glancing theme. But otherwise they bored me. I couldn't get interested. Fifty or a hundred pages were enough for tasting the style, and then I stopped. Now I have read both books with interest. I am not sure that I shall ever want to read them again. Jane Austen's *Emma* I have read ten times at the least. The first time ever so many years ago. I was in the gallery of the opera house in San Francisco, and the opera was *Aïda*. Its name is all I remember of it. My seat was at the edge and a little gas light burned over me continuously. I had begun with *Emma* before the opera started, and I doubt whether I ever knew that it did start. I have been reading *Emma* on and off ever since. I just read it again a few days ago. For a few minutes I had some doubts, I wasn't quite sure it was still a classic; but soon I was in it up to the neck, and the doubts were stilled. Some day, if I live long enough, I shall read again *The Wings of the Dove* or *The Golden Bowl*. My one reading assured me that they are candidates for classical honors. My next reading will tell whether or not they have passed. Despite this, I have little doubt that they are "classics."

Of course the case is different for the young and the old, for those with and those without experience; but it is not essentially different. One can learn like a man, not be trained like a beast, in so far as one has at once an open mind and a selective digestion. There are things that are at once convincing, and things that one must hold in abeyance. What one likes one should like despite the authorities, though one should be ready to change. I read the other day that Fitzgerald's *Omar Khayyam* is losing its contemporaneity—that its bloom as a "classic" is wilting, that it "dates." For some time I have felt this also. But I have vivid memories of other days when this was not at all true. I had by chance heard a couple of the stanzas quoted. In those days San Francisco had good book stores, but no copy of *Omar* was there, and I had to wait impatiently till one came from New York. Then, although I do not easily commit things to memory, I read this so constantly that soon I had it all by heart. A bookseller friend was about to publish a series of reprints, and asked me whether I had anything to suggest. I told him about *Omar*—which was printed from my copy in 1891, the first, I believe, of the numerous cheap reprints.

One will naturally have prejudices which both stand in one's way and act as stimulus. As a boy I was mad about Carlyle, and detested Ruskin. In my freshman year at Berkeley, I wrote an essay contrasting them and quoted from memory a passage from Carlyle as something quite opposed to Ruskinism. One should always verify one's quotations, for the instructor in English, Mr. Hubbard, showed me that I had inadvertently quoted not from Carlyle, but from Ruskin. I have long since become quite unable to read Carlyle—the quantity of noise is so in excess of the measure of sense—while Ruskin at his best is a delight.

So with time one builds up one's five-foot shelf. One

does not refuse the "classics." They always call upon you to try again, but as my father used to say to us when we were children and were to make up our own minds, "You're the doctor." A person who goes on indefinitely in a hazy state, reading dutifully more or less of the "classics" but never finding out whether they are classics or not, is not achieving culture. A man of real culture stands on his own ground. If he is honest, he will like some things that are "good" and some things that are "bad." I am amazed at the "blunders" committed by friends who are authorities of the first water, and they are amazed at mine. But we don't care. Be sure you're right, and then go ahead, says the proverb; but if in this field one wanted to be as sure as that, one would have to stick to Shakespeare and the Bible. I remember our surprise, many years ago, when Charles Eliot Norton in a lecture gave us the Bible and the *Golden Treasury* instead of the classic Bible and Shakespeare. Now not a little of the *Golden Treasury* goes into the discard. When that passionate Grecian, Thomas Love Peacock, lay dying, and someone would talk of current events, he said, "I want to hear no news less than two thousand years old."

Which ones of our contemporaries will make the grade we cannot say, but as we shan't be here even a hundred years from now to say "I told you so," we needn't worry about that. Someone sent me recently Untermeyer's anthology of recent American poetry. As I don't know one of the young poets from another, I can read them without bias, and I find some things in the book that I can read again and again. At the least, they are classic enough to last me overnight.

VI

Personal Adventures

WHAT happens is history; who makes it happen is a personal detail, though often an interesting and sometimes an important one. In what follows this detail is neither interesting nor important—at best occasionally amusing—but in order to happen at all it had to happen to someone, and as I am telling about it, I have to be in it. Autobiography is generally speaking not very reliable, less reliable even than history. The historian investigates his facts, the autobiographer just remembers them. When General Sherman was reproached for mistakes in his autobiography he answered, in effect, "That's the way I remember these things. Let those who remember them otherwise write what they remember, and so everyone will be pleased."

A queer thing in reading autobiographies in which one happens to appear, and in which much that is said about one is wrong because the writer didn't know enough of the affairs about which he writes, is that one still believes what the writer says of others. It is difficult to be skeptical when one has heard only an *ex parte* statement. There was the well-known judge who thought that there was no use of the second lawyer's speaking, since the first one had already convinced him. When one reflects, one can see that one is not a special case. But what can one do about it? To be so skeptical as to believe nothing, is to make the reading of the book useless. The most sensible way to read autobiographies is as Fiction and Truth—Dichtung und Wahrheit, as Goethe entitled his—that is, to read them for what they are worth. As authoritative documents, they are open to suspicion.

What follows is not precisely autobiography, though it is autobiographical. It is the story of certain adventures with art. It is based entirely on memory, as I have no documents. My memory is both good and bad, for though I forget much, I remember rather accurately what I have not forgotten. And then I like to verify, and always do it when this is possible. If a recollection is suspicious, I call up the context to see whether it fits. When I revisit a place in which I have not been for a long time, I inevitably look up everything I recall, to see whether it is as I recall it. When I reread a book I note the difference and the agreement with my previous impressions. Verification is a concession to my scientific spirit, even in matters of art. Therefore, I think that what follows is tolerably reliable.

My interest in pictures began early. Though I had no

precocious talent for drawing, I was always trying to draw, and pictures were important for me. In the eighties the *Century Magazine* was noted for its excellent illustrations, especially for its wood engravings by Kruell, Cole and others. After the numbers had been read I used to cut out these engravings and mount them. In California, in those days, pictures were not often to be seen. Occasionally one was exhibited, but very occasionally. One or two landscape painters had a local reputation, but if they ever had exhibitions I never heard of them. We had at home a volume of large scale line drawings of historical incidents, most of which I still remember. I recall with particular amusement a scene of armored knights with their families before a castle. This illustrated Luther's hymn, *Eine feste Burg is unser Gott,* A mighty fortress is our Lord—which I took to mean that you should put your trust in a mighty fortress as in God. I seem to have been even at that early age inclined to Napoleon's view that God is on the side of the stronger battalions.

Besides the panoramas of the battles of Waterloo and Gettysburg, I remember only four pictures: the *Constance de Beverly* by Toby Rosenthal, a Californian who had studied in Paris; a J. G. Brown; a Hudson School Niagara; and the *Man with a Hoe* by Millet. I talked with the painter of the Niagara, who explained to me how all the other Niagaras that had been painted were not the real thing, but his was. The Millet was the first picture I had seen that was done by a Famous Painter, and the local intellectuals were much exercised. We talked about nothing else for days. In fact, these were not absolutely the first pictures I remember, for I can recall one picture of a St.

Anthony plagued by Devils at the Belvidere in Vienna, which was then the picture gallery. Of the Louvre, which I must have visited in '78 or '79, I remember only the ship models and (curiously) most clearly of all, some links of a chain cable of the Great Eastern. When, many years later, I came again to Paris, I looked for the links and found them just as I remembered them, but with no label referring to the Great Eastern.

In '92 I left California to go to Harvard and spent as much time as I could in the Boston Museum, the Metropolitan, and the Walters Gallery in Baltimore, which had Chinese porcelains and a really choice collection of the Barbizon men. In '95 I came to Europe again. I had at this time the conviction that is characteristic of the young and serious student, that art should be pure and noble, that what isn't, isn't really art, and so on. I questioned *genre* and illustration. Therefore a picture in the Luxembourg illustrating the story of the quarreling donkey stealers, caused me qualms. It looked to me very good, and I came back to it again and again. But it was unquestionably a story-telling picture. It was by Daumier, whom I knew then only as a cartoonist. In time I came to know that there was no reason whatever why a painter should not tell a story if he could make a good painting of it, or even if he couldn't—provided he could make the story-telling sufficiently effective.

In time I ceased to be a purist, but at this moment I couldn't stay in Munich because it was so shoddy. There was imitation of everything. Once in a square I noticed that a building on one side of me was Corinthian, and a building on the other side was Ionic, and I said to myself,

"I bet the building behind me is Doric." Doric it was. There were Venetian palaces and Florentine palaces and an early basilica where, as I sprawled somewhat, looking at the painted beams of the openwork ceiling, a peasant woman scolded me for misbehaving in God's house. Wasn't I ashamed that an old woman like her must tell me so? Except the beer and the old Pinakothek, nothing in Munich pleased me—how those Rubenses reverberate in memory—so I fled to Dresden and its charming late Baroque and Rococo.

In Paris I spent every morning in the Louvre and much of the time in the Salle Carrée, at that time an epitome of the galleries, a selection of the masterpieces of all schools. My pet maxim then was, "Keep your eye on the object and let your ideas play about it." I always had plenty of ideas, though of course most of them came and went—for ideas in these matters that will stick are hard to find. Even Faraday said that ninety-nine ideas out of a hundred are no good. For a blissful month I looked and wondered "why," and then I had to go to Germany, and afterwards came back for another month in Paris, where I began to find things more intelligible. I was from the first obsessed by the notion of unity, for if one feels that somehow art is that pleasure which of all pleasures is most nearly related to essential satisfaction, then unity is all-important.

Goethe said: He who has art and science has religion; he who has not art and science let him get religion. The maximal religious condition is the mystical identification, a unity of self and whatever is or stands for God. There must be a unity with which to be unified, and when this is not the unity of everything, it must be represented by a unity which is its symbol. Every scientific law has to some extent this quality, and has this for its religious significance. Every work of art which is an achieved thing has this possibility, and though most works of art are too insignificant to suggest it, this possibility persists. So most scientific laws are too special to make one go so far afield.

But what I say is true for one who reflects and recognizes that the little and the big are in essentials equal, that the animals in a drop of water are as truly animals as the whale or the Brontosaurus. Newton's Law appealed as religiously significant to many who were not so impressed by the law of the pendulum or of gases. Men's minds need a strong reagent, and only thinking people think because they enjoy it. I recently read that an exchange professor, returning from England, said, "Believe it or not, English students think"—which seems to have been news in America. English soldiers who have been in contact with Americans are surprised to find that these almost never think of politics, though politics are for the moment the world's crucial matter. Thinking now and then is really not very bad for one; one can think in contraction about some particular business, or in expansion, and it is the expansive kind of thinking that I have here in mind.

There is in the Salle Carrée a huge picture of the *Marriage of Cana* by Veronese, a gorgeous thing with lots of people in splendid robes, backed by lofty classic architecture and a white-cloud-studded blue sky. During my first month in Paris, I couldn't make this picture come together, though I often tried. But when I had returned from Germany and came into the room, at the first glance I saw it as it had never been before—one and indivisible, as a picture ought to be. It was one, and I was one in the face of it. We were altogether one, and so something had been accomplished in the way of pictorial enlightenment.

My favorite picture in the Louvre was the *Crucifixion* by Mantegna, which to me seemed made of color as no other picture, even by the great Venetians or Rubens, was. This picture started me on the road which, when it arrived at Cézanne, made him familiar at first sight. Mantegna was born to be one of the greatest masters of color, but went to pot because instead of painting as nature said he ought to paint, he had ideas about this, and thought he ought to be a Roman. He ended by making rather ugly Roman statues in paint. This *Crucifixion* is one of the few pictures about which my feeling has never wavered. Most of the pictures, the Rembrandts, the Titians, the Velasquez and many others, have had their ups and downs, but that Mantegna has never budged.

I am also proud to have "discovered" the Rubens *Marie de Medici* decorations. At that time they hung in a never-ending line, in narrow frames, all the way down the long gallery, and were treated rather with contempt by the critics. It was only in 1900, when the present room was built, that they shone in all their glory and were generally seen. Those few months in Paris were radiant months for me and fixed my eventual interests, though I did a number of things before art became definitely the dominant one.

When in the fall I returned to America, it was to join a cousin with whom his father had invited me to go around the world. There were memorable moments on this trip: the first view of Fujiyama after nine days of storm at sea with all hatches closed; the wonder ride on the first evening ashore through the paper-lantern-lighted streets of Yokohama (for in '95 Japan was still to outer view the old Japan); then a couple of months of fascinating life in Kioto, which was out of bounds and where there were no foreigners; the strange accounts kept by Kai Inch with items like "trengobi"—which meant his ticket when we sent him to Kobe to find out whether Cleveland was going to war with Great Britain; Canton with its mysterious, keenly, almost ferociously intelligent-looking crowds; Ceylon, where I sat under a upas tree and survived, and where in Colombo I saw the streets, so Kiplingesque; Egypt, where more fascinating than the monuments were the gallops in the desert; Italy and the first taste of Naples, Rome, Florence, Venice; the trip through Vienna to Carlsbad, where I left my cousin with his family.

The world-encircling was richer for experience than for development, and when at the end of the summer I returned to America I was at loose ends. I tried biology for a while, but one day I got an idea that seemed fruitful for esthetics—something like what Croce turned out a few years later, and which he as a philosopher considered permanently important, but which I, with an interest in art and not in philosophy, soon came to regard as of little importance. Nonetheless, I decided to come to Europe and write a book on Mantegna. There was at that time no recent book on him in English, though two, it soon proved, were in the making, and appeared before I had time to look around much. Besides that, I found that my interest in art was esthetic and not historical; so I didn't want really to write it anyway. I spent two winters in Florence, and these were important for me for other reasons.

During those two winters I did the work I spoke of on seeing; I became really intimate with quattrocento Italian art—the art of Piero della Francesca, Paolo Ucello, Domenico Veneziano, Andrea del Castagno, and the early Siennese—and I discovered pragmatism. I was not the first to discover it. Charles Peirce had discovered it twenty years earlier; William James had given his California lecture two years before. At any rate, James says that pragmatism is just a new name for an old way of thinking; so it would seem that nobody really discovered it. But if it was never absolutely discovered, it was relatively discovered by me as well as by others. In philosophy as in art, it is more important to discover things for oneself. One has them then to satisfy felt needs. To be the first to make the discovery has social but not individual importance, and to insist on it is matter either of profit or pride.

I had naturally always been curious about philosophy, but I lacked the credulity that is necessary for the metaphysician. I couldn't make out just how it was that the different philosophers could be so skeptical when criticizing others, and so credulous when criticizing themselves. William James wanted a metaphysic as badly as anyone, but was too honest to shut his eyes to the no-thoroughfare signs, and remained, a bit uncertainly, on the outskirts. Most philosophers gave up the game at some point and crashed the gates. Others could catch them at it, as they could catch others, but they all refused to catch themselves. The history of philosophy is of course interesting, not for the solutions of the problems so much as for the study of the questions posed. I found in pragmatism a means of giving repose to my soul from the mysteries of metaphysics.

My pragmatism was a simple affair. It grew out of my attempt to find an intelligible meaning for identity—what sense could be given to A is B. I came to the conclusion that A is B whenever A could be put in place of B, could be substituted for it—which could be in any place except that of being opposed to B. Absolute identity was therefore not a puzzle, but a meaningless notion. I then came to the conclusion that nothing had a meaning that was not in some way limited, that had a context, and that therefore the Absolute, the central bastion in the philosophical battles of those days, was an illusion when considered a matter for thought. I finally came to a generalization that I called *presuppositions as hypotheses,* and which Schiller called axioms as postulates, which means that we start reasoning not with certainties but with things that we take for granted. There I stopped. If we have to remain in the world of the probable, I can't get any satisfaction in pretending that I'm in a world of certitudes. People often say that if they have no absolute beliefs, why should they not eat, drink and be merry, for tomorrow they die. The simple answer is that, generally speaking, we don't die tomorrow. We usually go on living for quite a while longer, and make the best of it. That is what I do, and quite cheerfully, though I know nothing whatever about God, Freedom or Immortality.

When I had got rid of philosophy as a bugaboo, I found in the works of some philosophers the literature that had been more or less concealed when one worried over their fallacies. I now read them as I read the Bible, the Buddhist Scriptures, or my special favorites, the *Gospel of St. Mat-*

thew and the *Tao Teh King* of Lao Tse. Kant is not amusing, but he is splendid as he goes through the seas of epistemology like a sea-shouldering whale, to use Chapman's impressive phrase. Leibnitz's *Monadology* is more thrilling than a whodunit. I never can remember it all, and each time I read, I get a thrill wondering how he's going to "get out of it." Berkeley's *Three Dialogues* combines ingenuity, ingenuousness and charm elsewhere unequaled; and Plato, whom I have just reread in Jowett's translation, is the perfect blend of the sweet, the sour, and the bitter of charm and irony and scorn. There is no finer prose than Schopenhauer's or Nietzsche's, which one can enjoy to the full if one will not quarrel with their ideas, but treat them as what they really are—writers of penetrating fiction.

Between my two winters in Florence, I spent a summer in Spain. I expected, of course, that my great sensation would be Velasquez, but I was disappointed. I had already begun my experiments in seeing, and wasn't in the least impressed by what Velasquez saw. His vision seemed to me utterly commonplace. Again and again I noticed that people who stood before his pictures, looking at them, were to me pictorially more interesting than the pictures they were looking at. Of course he could paint very well what he saw, and there was something of interest in that. Also, he could place a single figure in the canvas admirably, but this was hardly enough. I found Goya more satisfactory. At that date it was still possible to "discover" El Greco, but the pictures in the Prado were being rehung and the Grecos were not yet in place, and to Toledo I did not go. Both Gertrude and I suffered from insomnia on the high dry plateau of Madrid. Toledo was to come after Madrid, but suddenly in desperation we ran away to a more restful climate, and in Bordeaux we slept the clock around.

The winter of 1902 I spent in London, and there bought my first modern painting. While in Florence, I used to pick about in the junk shops as everyone does, but I had neither the patience nor the talent for fingering over the messes that one finds in them. I got one minor "masterpiece" for very little, but that was pointed out to me by a more talented friend. In London, it was another matter, for I bought an oil painting—just like that.

To have bought an oil painting may not seem like a remarkable thing to have done, but it was remarkable forty-odd years ago for one who was not rich. I had already bought etchings and Japanese prints, but when I bought that picture by Wilson Steer I felt a bit like a desperado. Oil paintings were for the rich: that was part of the American credo. A minor Parisian dealer told me that an American woman came into his shop and asked if he had any Raffaellis. He showed her what he had, and she liked one picture very much. She asked the price. Eight hundred francs—one hundred and sixty dollars.

"But then it isn't an original?" she queried.

He assured her he had it from Raffaelli himself. She was disappointed. She said that was not what she wanted; she wanted a picture for about a thousand dollars. So he sent her to Durand Ruel, where pictures were more expensive. My Wilson Steer cost me a good deal less than that Raffaelli. It wasn't in itself very important, but it was important to me as an encouragement. One could actually own paintings even if one were not a millionaire.

At the end of 1902, I left London rather hurriedly because I lacked diplomatic talent of even an elementary kind. At the Japan Society, to which I had been taken by Laurence Binyon, I met a very gracious old gentleman, a well-known writer on architecture. We came together several times and he asked me what I was doing on the near-approaching Christmas Eve. I said I had no intimate acquaintances in London; so I would do the same on Christmas Eve as on any other evening.

The good old man was horrified. To be alone on Christmas Eve? He couldn't bear the idea. I must come to his house. I said that would not do at all, that he would have his children and grandchildren there, that I was clumsy and unadaptable to such conditions, and would not fit in. But he said that he could not and would not let me be alone that evening, and that I must promise to come. As I expected to go across the channel before long, I said I would come if I were still in London. I left it the afternoon of the twenty-fourth of December.

Years later, I thought how simple it would have been to write a note, saying that friends had unexpectedly turned up and I would spend the evening with them. But deliberate lying, even of this diplomatic kind, never came easy to me. So, instead, I wrote a note announcing my departure. I did not intend to stay long in Paris; I was really on my way to Florence and America. *Diis aliter visum,* the gods decided otherwise, and I stayed.

One night when Pablo Casals and I were dining together, as we did once a week, I said to him that I felt myself growing into an artist. The leaven of pictorial vision was working. When I got back to the hotel, I made a rousing fire, took off my clothes, and began to draw from the nude. Then I spent a week drawing from the statues in the Louvre; after that, I went to Julian's. I kept on painting for a few years, but nothing came of it because of a neurosis. Years after, when I had cured the neurosis, I took up painting again. Here it is important only because it decided me to stay in Paris. A sculptor cousin had come to Paris a little earlier and had searched widely for a place to live. As I don't like apartment hunting, I said to him that doubtless he had taken the best he found: what was the next best? He said the next best was 27 Rue de Fleurus. So I settled at 27 Rue de Fleurus, which in time became famous. A romance was published some years ago about this place and the people who lived in it, but it was so very romantic and so little related to the facts that what follows will make a quite different narrative. My impression is that it is more veridical.*

In those old days the official salons were still taken seriously. All the American painters in Paris sent to them, and the younger ones, when they got a picture accepted, got drunk with joy or with alcohol or, more commonly, with both. The *vernissages* were great events, the first of the social season, and one saw there everybody who was anybody. Willy with his flat-brimmed top hat, his wife Colette, and Polaire, who had the slimmest waist in France, were a trio one can't forget. The old salon was full of pictures big enough to cover a wall, sprawling with pink nudes and landscapes painted with a kind of leaden color, espe-

* The manuscript for this book was in the hands of the publisher before Gertrude Stein's unexpected death.

cially the water and the foliage—impenetrable, one would think, to any radiations. The kind of thing that the salon was full of forty-odd years ago is dead as the mastodons, though a few frozen specimens of the one, as of the other, no doubt exist somewhere. One lives through epochs nowadays, even in a lifetime of moderate duration.

The new salon was livelier, and showed what was trying to be the art of the then today. There was a certain freshness and vivacity in many of the pictures, and yet they were somehow not art with a big A; they were essentially not complete things. What was the matter?

I used to say that they lacked form, but that is too easy and rather stupid. It takes at least two terms to make a formula, and so I stopped at this point in my writing to find one. I looked into an old French art review which had a yearly article on the salons with very good reproductions, to refresh my memories of the work of Simon, Cottet, Henri Martin, Ménard and others; and as I looked, I found what I wanted. In the preceding chapter I have spoken of the opposition of construction to composition—that in the art of building, engineering is construction and architecture composition, and so on. In this I found my formula: sufficient art is where construction and composition coincide. In this salon art, that does not happen. The composition is made out of constructional elements, but is not one with it, and the result is either illustration or decoration. In these art magazines, there are many other good reproductions of pictures in galleries and private collections, and the striking contrast in respect to composition and construction between this salon art and the good stuff showed that my formula worked. I had already written the third chapter in terms of composition only, and now rewrote it in terms of the two factors.

In Paris forty years ago I didn't have the formula, but I had the fact. I had, on first coming to Paris, bought of the little dealer who did not have Raffaellis for a thousand dollars, a little picture by Du Gardier of a woman in white with a white dog on a green lawn. It was a pleasant thing of no real importance, but I spent much time at the shop, talking and getting acquainted with art matters in Paris, and this purchase paid my entrance fee. But then there was nothing more to buy, and I was discouraged. Of course there was plenty of older stuff, but this was too expensive—and, besides, it was not what I wanted. I wanted an adventure. It was in the second year that Berenson, the well-known authority on Italian art, helped me. He was in Paris, and I told him of the dearth of art. He said, "Do you know Cézanne?" I said that I did not. Where did one see him? He said, "At Vollard's"; so I went to Vollard's, and was launched.

Of course, in my frequentations of the Rue Lafitte, then the center of the Parisian art trade, I often passed Vollard's. But there never seemed to be any exhibitions on, and through the doors one had a glimpse of something like a junk shop, with heaps of pictures on the floor and against the walls, but nothing to indicate that one would be welcome. Occasionally there was a queer picture on show in the window, but isolated queer pictures remain queer. Now, however, I boldly went in, and soon was quite at home. In fact, once when rummaging through a heap of pictures, I saw something that interested me and showed it to Vollard. He said, "Oh, where did you find that? I sold that picture a month ago and have been looking for it ever since." I went there often, for Vollard liked to ask questions and learn what you thought about things, sometimes about pictures and often about other matters as well. He didn't mind my turning things upside down, since they were already in that state, and so we got on nicely.

I have already said that for me Mantegna's *Crucifixion* was a sort of Cézanne precursor "with the color running all through it." Also the Tuscan quattrocentisti, especially Piero della Francesca and Domenico Veneziano, were an excellent preparation. I was quite ready for Cézanne, and before going to Fiesole for the summer, I bought a *Landscape* which is figured on page 218 of Barnes's book.* The composition is a good one, and the space handling for the most part even exceptionally good. It was altogether a good beginning.

That summer I passed more time with Cézanne than I did with the pictures in the Uffizi and the Pitti. I told Berenson how I had profited by his suggestion, and he told me that Charles Loeser, who lived in Florence, had a lot of Cézannes. I thought that strange, as I had often been at Loeser's house, but Berenson explained that the Cézannes were not mixed with the other pictures which filled his house, but were all in his bedroom and dressing room. Loeser, the son of Brooklyn's "Macy's," had come to Italy soon after leaving Harvard, and was a hardened collector. He collected everything—pictures, bronzes, faience, drawings, furniture, ivory-headed canes. Then he bought a villa and rebuilt it. Until his marriage, long after, he didn't

* *Art of Cézanne* by Albert C. Barnes.

live in it, but just had it for building. He said to me that a painter or a sculptor kept changing his work till it was satisfactory—why shouldn't one do the same thing with a building? It finally turned out an interesting amalgam of new and old.

He had begun buying Cézannes in the early days, when Vollard's was a kind of five-and-ten establishment, and had got together an interesting lot. Loeser was not an intellectual, and he insisted that the best critic of Italian art that he knew was his old cook Maria. He always showed her his last discovered Madonna, and when Maria said, "Si signore, that *is* the madonna," he knew that it was all right. But when she shook her head and said, "No signore, that is *not* the madonna," he was sure that the picture did not ring true. During the summer I spent many days with the Cézannes and could never get enough of them. Loeser is long since dead, but I saw the pictures again a few months ago, when a show of French painting was held in the Pitti. The pictures are about as they were, but I am not, and only one or two still seemed to me important.

When I got back to Paris after the Cézanne debauch, I was ready to look further. It was a queer thing in those days that one could live in Montparnasse and be entirely unaware of what was going on in the livelier world of Montmartre. Of course, one went there at times, but not for art. The only Montmartre art we knew was the posters: Willette, Leandre, Cheret, Steinlen. Whistler was the patron saint of the Americans, and poor Alfred Maurer, who was no more akin to Whistler than was Toulouse-Lautrec, tried to paint in pastel colors the fat whores of the Boul'Mich' that he adored. If Maurer had landed on the other mountain, far from the Americans, he would have been in his element and doubtless have succeeded. But these things came to him too late; they came when painters were "experimenting," and for him that was too late. The Americans, as I first knew them, were not experimenting; they were not even going abroad. Beyond the official salons, they knew nothing and had heard of nothing. So now, when I went forth from Montparnasse, I was a Columbus setting sail for a world beyond the world.

It was interesting to come into this situation. I had just heard of Cézanne, and of course I knew Renoir and the impressionists, whose work one saw at the Luxembourg and at Durand Ruel's, but I had never heard of Seurat and Van Gogh, both long since dead, or of Gauguin. Except for the Renoirs at Durand Ruel's, there was nothing current of importance at the known dealers. For me it was virgin soil.

The Autumn Salon was new, and I began there. I went again and again, until things began to take shape. I looked again and again at every single picture, just as a botanist might at the flora of an unknown land. Bonnard and Vuillard and Maurice Denis and Van Gogh, of whom there was a little retrospective, Dufrenoy, Laprade, Girieud, Matisse, Marquet, Vallotton, Valtat, Rouault—there were plenty of those now known, half-known or almost forgotten. Matisse made perhaps the strongest impression, though not the most agreeable. He was at this moment trying pointillism, the ugliest technique—to my thinking—ever invented. His pointillism was splotchy and messy, and though both his drawing and his color had a decisive quality of energy, the pictures were not satisfying. I learned a lot at this Autumn Salon, but I bought nothing.

The following spring I went through the Independents' as thoroughly as I had gone through the Autumn Salon. This time I bought two pictures—one by Vallotton, a talented and essentially witty painter, a Swiss who had started painting rather powerful portraits influenced by Holbein, but who ruined his promise by marrying a rich wife—which a painter can rarely afford to do. The other picture was a successful study of the nude by Manguin, really school of Matisse, but of a kind of Matisse that I had not yet seen; otherwise I should not have been so well pleased with this Matisse at second-hand. I made acquaintance with both the painters, and so began moving out of Montparnasse.

The autumn of this year was marked by something that was decisive. Matisse came out from pointillism with the *Femme au Chapeau*. It was a tremendous effort on his part, a thing brilliant and powerful, but the nastiest smear of paint I had ever seen. It was what I was unknowingly waiting for, and I would have snatched it at once if I had not needed a few days to get over the unpleasantness of the putting on of the paint. One was not yet accustomed to the smears that since then are the commonplaces of technique. It was almost worse than had been the splashy points.

A tempest raged at the Autumn Salon. Matisse was told that only because he was a member and had a right to exhibit was the picture admitted. The visitors howled and jeered. Even the most faithful supporter of Matisse, the socialist Sembat, would have none of it. Matisse came to the salon once only, and his wife never dared to come at all.

When Gertrude stopped in at the tiny gallery in Montmartre—where Mlle. Weill, the funny little squinting near-sighted old lady who sympathized with revolutionaries, good, bad or indifferent and showed their pictures to the few who were interested—she heard the sad tale of Matisse's amazed disappointment and his discouragement. Matisse had thought that this time he had played the ace of trumps, and apparently it would take nothing.

After the couple of days needed to get used to the smearing, I made an offer for the picture. I had been told when I bought the pictures in the spring that no one in France ever pays the catalogue price, and that I should always offer about two-thirds, which is the real price. That is what I had done, and it had seemed satisfactory. So I did the same now, but at the office they showed me a reply from Matisse, saying that he did not consider the price of five hundred francs excessive, and that he could not let it go for less than four-fifty. I said I did not consider the price excessive either, that I had simply conformed to custom, and that if Matisse wished to innovate, I was quite content to follow him. So I did, and I had bought my first Matisse.

The next thing was to meet the painter. Manguin took me there. Matisse was different from the other painters whom I had met through Vallotton and Manguin. Vallotton himself was witty and cynical, Manguin a man of the world who talked easily and fluently, the rest earnest, serious workers—each a personality but not distinguished or really interesting. Matisse was really intelligent. He was also witty, and capable of saying exactly what he meant when talking about art. This is a rare thing with painters, and it is what makes occasional sayings of Cézanne valuable. Matisse was at work on the *Joie de Vivre,* his first big decoration, and it was giving him no end of trouble.

In this, however, the picture was not exceptional—for all his pictures, for a long time to come, were to give him a lot of trouble. He liked giving his opinion, and he liked to hear the opinions of others. I do not know whether he ever followed their suggestions, but he always wanted to hear them. A fellow student told a most amusing story of the corrections hour, when for a while Matisse worked in the atelier of Carrière. Carrière went from one student to the other, casting occasional nervous glances toward Matisse's easel, and managed by a skillful maneuver to bypass it.

But Matisse wouldn't let him off. "Monsieur, you have not criticized my study."

Unable to escape, poor Carrière sat down in front of it and burbled, "Well, you know, of course not everybody sees things as everybody else does, and of course one can't judge fairly when one is not sure just how someone else sees things who sees them differently from the way one sees them, and in that case one might say the wrong thing if one said anything, since one isn't sure where the other person stands in relation to oneself," and so on. Finally, perspiring somewhat, he escaped without having committed himself. Matisse has great maturity, and the temper of the eternal pupil: he is always willing to learn anyhow, anywhere, and from anyone.

To my thinking, Matisse was by far the most important and essentially vital of the younger (no longer younger, though I still so think of them) painters. He did something new with colors—bold, brilliant, subtle. I had a picture by him of a girl with a yellow hat, in which the hat was specially to be remarked. I never could make out why those yellows did what they did. Renoir, colorist as he was, could not understand how Matisse controlled his intense colors and made them keep their places—foreground, middle ground, background—just as he wanted them.

Just how much Matisse came in time to understand all this, I don't know, but once in the early days he told me that Maurice Denis had in a book said that it was all calculated, whereupon he had led Denis up to one of his pictures and asked him to examine it minutely and tell him whether the feat of calculating all those relations would not be a far more extraordinary thing than composing them intuitively. On this confrontation, Denis admitted that it would be. The picture of the girl with the yellow hat was one that Matisse had determined to work on a long time, but after the first séance he could do nothing more with it. In a way it was "unfinished," but finished so far as his seeing for the moment went. Matisse is intuitive, he is intelligent, in his way he is as persistent as Cézanne himself; and his best compositions are full, complete, veritable pictorial finalities such as one rarely finds.

Matisse was religiously conscientious about his work. He once showed me a picture that he had tried to make into a best seller when he was particularly hard up, but he couldn't see it through. After I had seen it, he put it on the floor and broke it with his heel. He worked endlessly on his pictures, and wouldn't let them go till they were finished. Once a picture had been ordered, and when the people who had given the order came to Clamart and saw it, they were pleased, and wanted to carry it off at once. But the picture was not finished. I happened to be there at the moment, and when the visitors had gone Matisse said sadly that no doubt when it was finished they wouldn't want it; and that was exactly what happened. I told Matisse that the next time he had better sell the "sketch," and begin the "picture" over again. As late as 1914, he showed me an interior with goldfish and said how he hoped in time to be able to finish freshly and at once, but that as yet painting was as difficult as ever. Norman Douglas told me once that every sentence he wrote was as painful as having a baby, and for a long time something of the sort was true of the pictures of Matisse. Later he did come to paint swiftly and decisively.

During the three years that followed on the *Woman with the Hat* I bought a number of Matisses—the last one, *The Blue Woman,* now in the Cone collection in Baltimore, but really a pink woman in blue scenery. Then I brought several pictures to the house for consideration, but did not keep any. For the moment they no longer served me.

It was the rhythm in Matisse that I found insufficient. Art is composition, and the life of composition is rhythm. Rhythm is movement, and where there is no movement it has to be as though there were movement. This is of necessity the case with painting, sculpture and architecture. As the things don't move, the movement must be suggested. I long ago came to think that perhaps the profound importance of rhythm depends on the feeling of recovery from a fall. It is often suggested that the feeling for rhythm depends on experience of the change of seasons, the movement of the sun and moon and stars, or on the pulse and breath, but this does not seem plausible. The former rhythms are too slow, and the latter are not attended to.

Man is a two-legged animal, but not, like the birds—who can sleep comfortably on their legs—a perfect biped. When he walks, he falls forward and arrests his fall by putting one leg before the other. Often he gets tired, and is very conscious of this. By stressing the footfall he gets the march and the dance, perhaps the most primitive of the arts. There is an acute pleasure in falling, if one is confident of recovery, as swings and gravity railroads prove. It happens that Watson found the fear of falling to be the primitive fear, and to fall indefinitely in dreams is terrible, but to swoop down and up is delightful. I don't claim that my thesis is demonstrably true, but it is suggestive, and in so far useful.

Obviously no rhythm can exist for one who does not in some way participate. A dancing figure would be only a figure moving from place to place, if there were no participation. We all know how natural it is to beat time, to sway, to show with our hands and feet that we too are artists of a kind. However secondarily we do it, we are participants.

In the case of sculpture, painting, architecture, where the objects are entirely at rest, we must supply all the real movement. People who look at pictures as mere representation are not bothered by this, but those who want rhythm have to do something about it. I happen to want it very much. I often said that there were only two arts for which I had a natural aptitude, cooking and dancing. My father was somewhat eccentric, and once discharged the cook because he wanted his daughters to learn cooking. So we all turned into the kitchen. Everything Gertrude tried to cook turned out badly, but I made bread and apfelstrudel—which is very difficult—and invented new pies and pancakes which were actually eaten.

My dancing I did mostly in private, quite by myself, developing combinations of rhythms. When on one rare occasion, having absorbed enough preliminary alcohol, I did some imitations of Isadora Duncan, a young lady who was present said, "It is too beautiful to be burlesque," and she wrote a poem about it. Rhythm is my element, rhythm and space. Composition suggests the way we should inwardly move in response, and the result depends on our capacity to deal with wholes.

We are somewhat like the strings of a violin, and a picture is the bow that sets us in motion. Just as a bow may become too smooth and fail to bite on the strings, or the strings may lose their elasticity, so it is with pictures and ourselves. A rhythm that is too obvious may cease to stimulate—or one that is too simple. Other things in the picture, technical qualities that once interested, or illustrative ones, drama or religious meanings, may grow stale; the picture may thus become a more purely formal thing, and we may make more demand on these formal characters. Esthetically untrained people are bored by the endless madonnas in the great galleries, which were painted when the audience was more interested in madonnas, though even then they may not have cared for so many in a row. Today it is necessary to be interested in those pictures with little reference to the original intention, or else not to be interested at all.

It happened to me over and over again that I lost interest in very good pictures when the novelty of the kind of thing which had before been genuinely interesting wore off, and that I then demanded of them the qualities that made important pictures which had not these novel values. Cézanne did magnificently certain things. Renoir said of him that he could not put colors together at all without making a picture. In the early days I often tore a little hole in a piece of paper and moved it about on a painting enjoying these little compositions. Also, Cézanne rarely fails in bringing fragments of his pictures to tolerable completion, or in getting a whole carried to a certain point. But to get that whole to the stage where I can rest in it content is, I find, anything but common with him; in fact, it is uncommon.

Cézanne would probably have agreed. He deplored his incapacity to "realize," and once said of pictures that he considered insufficient, "And really, they admire that stuff in Paris?" I also deplore it, and see no reason why I should be more easily satisfied than he. Occasionally the thing comes off and a masterpiece results, but masterpieces in painting, as in the other arts, are not common. It happens in those arts where the original can be known in reproduction, especially literature and music, that we can all have the best and ignore the rest, whereas in painting the original is unique and one puts up with what is inferior.

The practice I have spoken of, seeing compositions in nature, is an education unlike any other. I can look out at the window in any direction, here where I am now writing, from my bedroom, from the kitchen, from the bathroom, and see things that no one could adequately render. There is nothing remarkable to be seen from any of these windows

—no "views," no perspectives, no panoramas. If I go upstairs I can get all those things—splendid ranging hills, Florence with its cupolas and towers, one side clustered under Settignano, the other sweeping into the plain that looks toward the distant Pisan mountains, a marvelous picture.

But though I can revel in all this, I have no need to go upstairs, for the contracted space here below—with a few olive trees, some buildings, piles of faggots, bits of green field and stone wall—are "dukedom large enough." The rhythms that I can draw out of, or put into, what I see, are so tremendous and so vital, that I cannot find as more than casually interesting what in art is less—for I do not take art either as a business or a ritual. The space in Cézanne's landscapes is rarely a complete rhythmic realization. His figure things are almost always fragments. His incomplete portrait of Vollard after a hundred and fifteen sittings is typical of this. The nothings that I spoke of as seeing from my windows, I have been looking at daily for six years, and they are more wonderful than ever. But in the six years from the time I bought that first Cézanne, I had had enough of intensive concern with so-called modern art. I had come to find it only very occasionally good enough.

From this excursus on rhythm, I return to Matisse. After three years I could not buy any more of his pictures, for they were rhythmically insufficient. I was always interested to see what he was doing, because he always kept moving and generally moved forward; but it was enough for me to see his pictures at exhibitions. Only when I came to Paris after the first war did I see something that was more than interesting.

Matisse had a show in 1920. None of the pictures seemed

to me especially important, but there was also on show a little drawing on a scrap of torn paper, a girl at the piano, which I thought essential. There was something in it that I had never seen before in a work by Matisse, something pointing toward a greater significance. That evening I spoke to my sister-in-law, who was intimate with Matisse, and told her my impressions of the drawing. She said that Matisse had talked to her about this drawing and had said that if he could do in paint what he had done in this sketch he would be doing what he really wanted to do.

The great result predicted in the drawing was not immediately attained, but in time it was—not constantly, but often enough to prove the master. In '39 was published a volume of color reproductions of Matisse's pictures, and among these are a few that are completely satisfying. Matisse may fairly be counted as a fortunate man, who has accomplished his destiny.

VII

More Adventures

It was later in the year I met Matisse that I met Picasso. I had known for some time in the Rue Lafitte a little dealer, an ex-clown with a pointed beard and bright eyes and a hat pushed back on his head, who twinkled with enthusiasm whatever was the subject, but especially when that subject was Zan or current painting. Zan was a particular brand of licorice which was different from any other and the only one that had the properties of a life-preserver. He would interrupt the talk on modern art to put a bit of Zan between his teeth and commend its virtues; then we were back again on the latest show, the latest artistic scandal, the prospects for the future. There was a Spaniard whose works he lauded, and as he had done me some favors I bought a little Spanish water-color; but when he recommended another Spaniard, I balked.

"But this is the real thing," he said. So I went to the exhibition, and in fact this was the real thing. Besides the pictures, there were some drawings for which I left an offer, since there was no one in charge of the show, but from this I heard nothing further. When, a few days later, I dropped in at Sagot's to talk about Picasso, he had a picture by him, which I bought. It was the picture of a mountebank with wife and child and an ape. The ape looked at the child so lovingly that Sagot was sure this scene was derived from life; but I knew more about apes than Sagot did, and was sure that no such baboon-like creature belonged in such a scene. Picasso told me later that the ape was his invention, and it was a proof that he was more talented as a painter than as a naturalist.

Soon after, I learned that a friend, Pierre Roché, knew Picasso. Roché, a tall man with an inquiring eye under an inquisitive forehead, wanted to know something more about everything. He was a born liaison officer, who knew everybody and wanted everybody to know everybody else. He introduced me to the literary band at the Closeries des Lilas—Jarry, Moreas, Paul Fort and others who had recently made literary history—and once a month or so he came to see me, to tell his news and hear mine. We talked the whole night through. I was always having ideas, and as the same neurosis that kept me from painting kept me from writing also, it was nice to have someone like Roché, who was more ear than anything else. He was delighted to know that I had seen the work of Picasso, and a few days later led me to the Rue Ravignon.

One could not see Picasso without getting an indelible impression. His short, solid but somehow graceful figure, his firm head with the hair falling forward, careless but not slovenly, emphasized his extraordinary seeing eyes. I used to say that when Picasso had looked at a drawing or a print, I was surprised that anything was left on the paper, so absorbing was his gaze. He spoke little and seemed neither remote nor intimate—just quite completely there. The impression he made was satisfying. He seemed more real than most people while doing nothing about it. The atelier was a mess. There was a heap of cinders beside the round cast-iron stove, which was held together with a twisted wire (it later burst); some crippled furniture; a dirty palette; dirty brushes; and more or less sloppy pictures. Long after many of the pictures had become mine, Picasso came to the house one day with his paint box and cleaned them up. Later Vollard bought a bunch of them on condition that he should do the same for him, but I believe he never did.

The homes, persons and minds of Picasso and Matisse were extreme contrasts. Matisse—bearded, but with propriety; spectacled neatly; intelligent; freely spoken, but a little shy—in an immaculate room, a place for everything and everything in its place, both within his head and without. Picasso—with nothing to say except an occasional sparkle, his work developing with no plan, but with the immediate outpourings of an intuition which kept on to exhaustion, after which there was nothing till another came. The difference in mental type between Picasso and Matisse came out vividly in a later incident.

At Durand Ruel's there were at one time two exhibitions on, one of Odilon Redon, and one of Manet. Matisse was at this time specially interested in Redon, because of his own work and because of friendship with the older man, who was then in difficulties. When I happened in he was there, and spoke at length of Redon and Manet, with emphasis on the superior merits of the lesser man. It was quite common for Matisse, whose mind was not rigid, to overflow in some direction because of a temporary interest. He told me he had seen Picasso earlier, and Picasso had agreed with him. This seemed to me improbable. Picasso's appreciations did not have this fluidity, and he had no special interest in Redon. However, there was no reason to say this, so I let it pass.

Later on that same day Picasso came to the house and I told him what Matisse had said about Redon and Manet. Picasso burst out almost angrily, "But that is nonsense. Redon is an interesting painter, certainly, but Manet, Manet is a giant." I answered, "Matisse told me you agreed with him." Picasso, more angrily: "Of course I agreed with him. Matisse talks and talks. I can't talk, so I just said *oui oui oui*. But it's damned nonsense all the same." Picasso, though often influenced by others, was not so openly receptive as Matisse was.

Matisse was a social person rather than a convivial one. Picasso was more convivial than social. Matisse felt himself to be one of many, and Picasso stood apart, alone. He recognized others, of course, but as belonging to another system. There was no fusion. Matisse exhibited everywhere.

He always wanted to learn, and believed there was no better way than to see his work alongside the work of everybody else. Picasso never showed with others. It was partly diffidence, partly pride. Once at a salon he said to me, "I don't see how these fellows can exhibit this stuff; of course my work is bad too, but then I know it"; after a moment, "Perhaps they know it too, but they show because it's the best they can do."

Renoir once said, "I want to remain in the ranks"—something Picasso could never have said. He felt himself a man apart—what the story books call a man of genius, though not pretentiously so. But in those days he was not sure. He was not aggressive, but felt the right to be aggressive. Once we were waiting for places in an omnibus, and many went on. After the passengers with lower numbers than ours had mounted, Picasso burst out, "This is not the way it ought to be. The strong should go ahead and take what they want." But he was not very sure. When he had something in his head he could easily put it forth, but when he was fallow there was nothing behind. Matisse often felt uncertain, but he never felt empty. He was eternally revolving the artist's eternal problem: how to realize (to use Cézanne's favorite term). This did not trouble Picasso. He had always been an illustrator, and when he had his theme he could easily develop it.

Once when I said to Berenson that Picasso had a vital personality, he answered, "Perhaps, but not an artistic personality." In an important sense that was true and is still true. His personal feeling is more important than his personal form, and this has made it possible to be the greatest trick artist known without falling into emptiness. He has not had an organic development. His taste is impeccable (his fatal good taste, as someone has called it); he has a grace like that of Raphael, which is pervasive and perhaps his greatest real esthetic asset; he has humor, fancy, both light and tragic, invention, an abundant supply of qualities. He would have been a truly great artist, I think, if he had been more genuine; as it is, he's an extraordinary phenomenon. At the moment when I met him, he was at his best and made on me a strong impression.

After meeting Picasso I went again to Sagot's. Gertrude was with me this time and Sagot showed us a picture of a nude, almost naked little girl with a basket of red flowers. I liked the picture, but Gertrude hated it. A few days later I bought it. That day I came home late to dinner, and Gertrude was already eating. When I told her I had bought the picture she threw down her knife and fork and said, "Now you've spoiled my appetite. I hated that picture with feet like a monkey's." Some years after, when we were offered an absurd sum for the picture and I wanted to sell it—since for that money one could get much better things—Gertrude would not agree to sell, and I believe that she always kept it.

From this time on I saw Picasso often, either at the Rue Ravignon or the Rue de Fleurus. He was then in the last months of the Harlequin Period, painting acrobats and mountebanks. His inspiration had not yet run dry, for the best things of the period came then: *The Boy Leading a Horse,* and the large composition with a group of people, which I think was the last. With this period's end came an end to more than one of his characteristic periods; it was the end of an epoch in his life. It was Cézanne's fault, or rather the fault of Cézanne's reputation. Hitherto Cézanne had been important only for the few; he was about to become important for everybody. At the Autumn Salon of 1905 people laughed themselves into hysterics before his pictures, in 1906 they were respectful, and in 1907 they were reverent. Cézanne had become the man of the moment.

Matisse said once that Cézanne is "the father of us all," but he did not reckon with the phoenix Picasso, who had no father. Yet Cézanne could not be ignored. It was no longer a time for illustration, and Picasso for the first time tried for something that was not illustration at all: the result was deplorably feeble. This was the pink period, Picasso at his weakest. He did figures that were just figures, and there was hardly enough to them to make them worth doing. It was at this moment that I suggested he try working from the model in order to get more stuff into his figures. He came to my studio twice, but could make nothing of it; the few drawings he made did not, so to speak, look at the model. He also worked on Gertrude's portrait, but could not finish that.

Picasso's interior resources were too small for his then needs, and he had to have support from the outside. He found it in Negro art, which was a kind of substitute for an illustrative subject. With this he managed to "finish" Gertrude's portrait while we were away in Fiesole; though, as he left all except the mask as it had been before, the picture as a whole is incoherent. An artist, like a business man, needs a working capital; and if he can't make it by his own exertions, he has to borrow it. Picasso now borrowed it from the Negroes and it kept him going for a while. His forms grew bigger and in intention more powerful, but the reality was less than the appearance. I was not seriously interested in this stuff, but I was in his talent. Nor did I trust his morale. I often said that I had complete confidence in Matisse, who would give all that was possible for him to give, but that the future of Picasso was unpredictable, as there was no assured center. His present way was a makeshift, and to it there was no future that was inevitable. Of course with his talent he could make something of it as he could of anything, and in hopes of something better I bought a few of these Negroid things. Matisse was once looking at one of them with the patient earnestness with which he always studied the work of his contemporaries, and at length he spoke. "Ye-es, it's very ni-ice, very ni-ice, but—isn't it just the same thing?" Of course what Matisse meant was that though the forms were larger and the curves more sweeping, the forms were not really any bigger than they had been. In spite of the pretense, the difference was only a matter of illustration.

Picasso was pleasantly childlike at times. I had some pictures relined, and Picasso decided that he would have one of his pictures too treated like a classic, though in reverse order—he would have the canvas lined first and paint on it afterwards. This he did on a large scale, and painted a composition of nudes of the pink period, and then he repainted it again and again and finally left it as the horrible mess which was called, for reasons I never heard, the *Demoiselles d'Avignon*.

A revolutionary moment succeeded. Picasso began to have ideas. Bergson's creative evolution was in the air with its seductive slogan of the *élan vital*. There was a friend of the Montmartre crowd, interested in mathematics, who talked about infinities and fourth dimensions. Picasso began to have opinions on what was and what was not real, though as he understood nothing of these matters the opinions were childishly silly. He would stand before a Cézanne or a Renoir picture and say contemptuously, "Is that a nose? No, this is a nose," and then he would draw a pyramidal diagram. "Is this a glass?" he would say, drawing a perspective view of a glass. "No, this is a glass," and he would draw a diagram with two circles connected by crossed lines. I would explain to him that what Plato and other philosophers meant by "real thing" were not diagrams, that diagrams were abstract simplifications and not a whit more real than things with all their complexities, that Platonic ideas were worlds away from abstractions, and couldn't be pictured, but he was bent now on doing something important—reality was important whatever else it might be, and so Picasso was off.

The first attempts were not at all novel. In fact, they were just like the diagrammatic reductions of heads that one finds in books on drawing, like those in Haddon's *Figure Drawing,* for instance. But Picasso did not stop there; he went on and on. He and Braque worked together, and, as Braque wrote later, tried to be absolutely impersonal and absolutely original. All kinds of speculative funny business and shorthand went into the making, until finally the subject was ignored, except as a suggestive starting point.

Picasso had now what in view of his lack of essential seriousness he needed. It is possible that if he had not found a system he would in time have gone to pot. Mere drifting and waiting for inspiration might have soured, and Picasso might have taken to drink or something worse.

The exercise of ingenuity was a safeguard. As Margaret Kennedy says somewhere, "Ingenuity is perhaps the most satisfactory exercise in the world for the human brain. It keeps man happy much longer than inspiration can."

It does more than that—it stimulates inspiration, at least inspiration of a kind, just as rhymes may do when one is writing verse. In my younger days I sometimes suffered from insomnia, and would talk to myself in rhyme, generally in the meter of, "Here comes Poe with his raven like Barnaby Rudge, Three-fifths of him genius and two-fifths sheer fudge." Once it got well under way, the difficulty was to stop it, for the rhymes would carry on almost of themselves. So it is with Picasso's inventions. Often the end of one picture is the beginning of the next. When I say that Picasso was essentially not serious, I do not mean to say that he did not feel serious. Of course he did. But to take inventions for something else is essentially not being serious. Picasso had no longer the need of intervals of recharging. His inventive genius was constantly productive, and served as a sufficient stimulus to his feelings to give them an outlet. Picasso was at this critical moment being an intellectual, which may have been a saving grace for him on the whole, but was otherwise unfortunate—unfortunate because it is a real misfortune when a man of great talent must depend on a low-grade intellectuality.

Another of the great truths excogitated at this time was the definition of a head. A head, he told me, was a matter of eyes, nose, mouth, which could be distributed any way you like—the head remained a head. And so Picasso made innumerable heads on this novel pattern, sometimes throwing in some hair and teeth for good measure. The nose, which was the starting point of all this, is never ignored, though often reduced to two dots which are, I suppose, the nostrils. But the ears are never given. Perhaps Picasso considered them as mere appendages not worthy to enter into this world of reality.

Picasso did not stop at re-creating the head, he re-created the body also. Call a thing a woman, and a woman it is—and you profit by what I have called the dimensionality of sex. He made the most marvelous women and many other marvelous things. They got sometimes to be so queer that even he could not recognize them, but he told me that the faithful disciple and dealer, Kahnweiler, was never at fault. He could always tell what they were.

The fantastic contraptions invented by Picasso had no limit. If it was not one thing, it was another; it came rather close to being everything. Besides cubistic analyses and syntheses, there were scrapbag assemblages like *The Three Musicians,* in which more or less real people, or those who could pass as such, were made up of odds and ends. With his extraordinary powers as an illustrator, he could give considerable expressive values to the most extravagant fantasies, and any chance suggestion could revive him if for the nonce he had exhausted the present stock. Of course I have no idea what were the suggestions for the more than fifty-seven varieties of Picassian fantasticalities, but it does seem to me almost incredible that a public could have been found to take seriously this odd stuff simply because Picasso was a man of talent.

Picasso himself declares that he ought to be accepted for this reason. One of the quotations from him in Gertrude's book says that though people admit that he can draw like

Raphael, they want to stop him from doing what he likes. Picasso's argument might have been valid if these things had been the genuine intuitions of an artist, but they were not. I know that they were not because we talked of these things again and again, and I heard Picasso's reasons.

Even where there is a blackberry plenty of reasons, few will be so absurd as were Picasso's. If he had not had these reasons and had none the less been able to develop, his development would have been saner. He would have been less of a sensation but perhaps a more serious artist. Some people do not agree with me, and find his intellect impressive. Henry McBride speaks of the intellectual keenness of the things that Gertrude quotes from Picasso. After reading this opinion, I read them through again carefully, and I will say that either McBride or I is no judge of intellectual keenness, for I can find no trace of such a thing. Picasso is no fool—anything but it. He is observant and often shrewd. He is humorous and can wisecrack on occasion, but having significant thoughts is quite another matter, and having one's direction determined by ideas is altogether a serious matter for an artist. It is to subject his essential purpose to the direction of his intellect, and it would seem to me that any sane person looking at the result could see how absurd it was in this case.

There is one expression of Picassian intellectuality so extraordinary that I must put it in here. His friend Cocteau is the authority for it. A decoration for the theater was being made, and Picasso strode up and down before a large white wooden panel. Suddenly he stopped and rubbed red chalk on it. Then with ink he blackened some places and three columns leaped to view. This apparition startled those present, and they applauded. In the street, on leaving, Cocteau asked whether this had been calculated or whether it came as a surprise. Piscasso answered that it was unexpected, though one, no doubt, calculated without knowing it. He added that as he had invented these columns, so perhaps had the Greeks discovered the Doric column.

All this was very surprising. I wondered whether the words could mean something different from what they seemed to mean. Was it possible that one should so fatuously confound reminiscence and invention? Whether possible or not, here it was done. This is especially amusing when one remembers how pronounced the tendency to reminiscence was in Picasso. Picasso was continually playing variations on other people's themes—sometimes with intention, sometimes without. Stephan Bourgeois says that Picasso has a powerful intellect. Sample it anywhere, and this is about the way it works. A powerful imagination if you will, but intellect never.

Picasso was incapable of any intensive study of form. When he tried to make his forms big, he gave his figures elephantiasis. In this respect he was entirely different from Matisse. Manguin told me that a group of students was not satisfied with the week's pose, because it did not give them time enough for thorough study. So they got a pose for a month, but Matisse was the only one who stuck it out. Not only that, but yet dissatisfied, he got the same model to pose in the same position for a statuette, and worked on it for three years with more than a hundred sittings.

Some years later, Matisse did a similar thing with a female torso, which was cast in plaster and kept to be reworked every little while. Picasso, when he worked a long time, was busy with a remaking. The *Demoiselles d'Avignon* began as one thing and went through many phases, ending as a mixture of all sorts of things. In the powerfully effective *Guernica,* the research was for effectiveness of composition and expression, not for form.

In the Museum of Modern Art catalogue it says that "Picasso's ability to breathe new life and charm into a style so exhausted by overuse as the neo-classic is demonstrated by the *Woman in White.*" This statement, which is quite correct, is made pretentiously impressive by conventional habits of thought. Picasso's almost specific ability is to breathe life and charm into things. Why not into what anyone may be pleased to call the neo-classic? After all, that means no more than a rather linear painting of a woman with a Greekish head. Most people would make that dull, just as they make dull a Cézanne still life or a cubist concoction. Breathing life and charm into things is what made me take to Picasso in the first place, and if he had gone on doing this with increase of passion and of power as he matured, my interest would have continued and doubtless grown. But when he became an intellectual at a contemptible level of degradation I couldn't accept it. Of course his talent didn't die, it became in fact more mature. There is more power of expression and design in later work than in the earlier. It is not the lack of ability that puts me off, but the silliness. It is not abstract ability that makes for interest in a work of art, but competence applied to good purpose. What one wants, at least what I want, is a certain total result.

I have already said that full appreciation is a re-creation

by the observer. If the observer in question is me, he is a person of a given intelligence and culture. My plenary reactions have to be mine and not those of another. If there is to be an intellectual expression I want the intellect to be valid. If there is to be primitivism, I don't want it to be childish. I like primitive art of a kind. All rhythm is basically primitive, and when this basic power is manifest through all developments, one has primitivism at its greatest sufficiency. I know nothing more primitive than the theme of Beethoven of which I spoke when treating of seeing. I know nothing more primitive than Michelangelo. The more basic power there is in the expression, the more I realize its essential primitiveness. But I prefer this primitiveness expressed either as pure barbarism or at my own level of intelligence and culture, and not at that of chambermaids, bus drivers, and *douaniers*.

The first time I saw the work of Rousseau at the Independents', I recognized a talent, a gift for composition and color, but I don't want that sort of thing hanging on my wall and staring me in the face all the time. I like to talk with the people of the village, but I don't want to live with them. After I had talked with one who had some interest in art and ideas, he told my wife that it was as though he had passed out of the provinces into the great world. He was as good a man as I was—in some ways that I can recognize he is better—but what is for him the upper ether is my dwelling place. With Picasso as a man, and an artist, well and good, but with Picasso as a thinker there's nothing doing.

Picasso may have given up "thinking." In the discourses printed in the Modern Museum catalogue he speaks of himself as a pure intuitive. It is quite possible that this is true now, though I put little faith in the introspections of the uncritical. By thinking he got himself shunted onto the track which led into the beyond where his ingenuity could have full play, and the results of that thinking are all over the place. It is quite possible that no more thinking is necessary. Every fantasy has rights of citizenship, and his incredible facility could make something of it. There is in this nothing to quarrel with. These things apparently satisfy Picasso and many are enthusiastic over the results. The editor of the Modern Museum catalogue can tell us with a straight face that No. 231 is a most important painting of the Bone Period. Picassian archeology may some day be the occasion of professorial chairs. But I chuckle as I read. *Suum cuique,* if everyone could get his own, all the world would be happy, at least for a little while, and Picasso seems to have made no inconsiderable contribution to what some people want.

Picasso and Braque invented, contrived, excogitated, or educed cubism. I am not sure what the proper word is, but Picasso says it was not "researched." I doubt, however, whether he has ever applied his thinking powers to the elucidation of this word. Research may mean that you are after something that you foresee, as people were looking for the atomic bomb, or it may mean that you are following certain clues to see what they will lead to. In that sense Picasso and Braque were researchers. When once you know that a nose is not a nose is not a nose you can go on to discover what all the other things are not, and arrive at the conclusion that the way to build up "real" things is out of "the broken fragments of a once glorious union, of states dissevered, discordant." But when the analysis is only a kind of funny business, the synthesis will be only another kind of funny business. With this kind of funny business analysis, anything can be analyzed into any elements, and with this funny business synthesis any elements can be synthesized into any form. The analysis and the synthesis alike are mere funny business, and it is absurd to take them seriously.

Among other great ideas unfolded were the simultaneity of aspects and the intersection of planes. "Back and sides go bare, go bare," says the old song, and the simultaneists proceeded to put this into effect, and lay bare the concealed aspects of things. Metzinger and others painted pitchers cut in two down the middle, with one-half facing outward, and the other in profile. I don't think that Picasso ever did anything quite so silly, but to a naïve human being like myself it seems obvious that the back and sides of a figure even seen from the front are made more real when the object is realized in deep space than when some fragmentary hints are given of what one would see if one peeped round the corner.

Picasso had no command of deep space, as he had none of substantial form. I once pointed out to Mr. Sam Lewisohn that two Picassos which hung on a wall with other pictures, one early and one late, but neither one a cubist picture, were shallower than any other of the others. The simultaneity of aspects amounts to nothing more than a slightly stereoscopic effect, as in some of Picasso's later heads, or the fact that forms suggested by the object can be used for compositions. Of course, Picasso, with his great talent for composition, often so used the elements delightfully. Also one can get other-dimensional suggestions. I use the word dimension, as I have used it for sex, to mean effective values in art which are incommensurable with others. For instance, when bits of violins, guitars, notes suggestive of music, are introduced, the dimension of music is added to the formal composition. Sometimes this is effective, and sometimes not. The notion can be applied with anything that has suggestiveness, like Poussin's well-known *Et in Arcadia Ego* or Picasso's less familiar *J'aime Eve,* or someone's visiting card. Braque too arrived at something that was quite successful in the application of the method of more or less fragmentation when he did those little still lifes with fruits and nuts and tableware.

Intersecting planes seem to me to be entirely without justification. Long before cubism, it had seemed to me reasonable that if the subject did not count, one might make pictures entirely abstract, and I made a number of drawings on that assumption in 1906. But I found that when lines and planes intersected, they became confused, and the composition lost determinate character, and could be read in different ways. In Cézanne the planes do not intersect, but interlock. When better artists than I took up this thing, I was interested to see what they could do to avoid this confusion. But they seemed to revel in it. I am interested to see that in the linear drawings illustrated in the Museum catalogue (No. 205 a) Picasso has put knots at the intersection of the lines and thus preserved a certain order.

In an interesting book which chance brought to my notice, *Architecture, Time and Space,* I saw pictures of Picasso and other cubists put parallel to buildings and significantly related. So far as I could see, the comparisons were only schematic. In the buildings, the spatial relations suggested and those seen were the same. In the pictures, they were only told about. Many people today as in former days look at pictures for what they say rather than for what they are. Then, stories and sentiments were read; today, the reading is of formal relations. The authenticity in one case may be no greater than in the other.

No one with a sense of realities can set up as a judge in matters esthetic. I have not the slightest idea what other people, who find admirable the portrait of Kahnweiler or the *Pierrot* of the Guggenheim Foundation, see. If they see something I don't see, they have the advantage of me; if they see no more and get some satisfaction out of it, then their interests are other than mine. In 1911 or 1912 Gertrude bought a cubist Picasso, the first picture for which she was responsible to come to 27 Rue de Fleurus. I looked at it often, and it always remained the confusion that it was at the beginning. I have of course seen a lot of them, and find these mixed-up ones as futile to contemplation as I find the ideas underlying them to be silly. The so-called analysis is a mere make-believe of analysis, and the synthesis a half-correlated correlation between an intention in respect of the object and decorative exigencies. Picasso admitted this when I asked him the reason for certain lines in some early work of that kind. I also once asked him the reason for some wavy shading all over the place. He said that didn't mean anything except a sort of completion, since the lines which were the real picture were too bare. Later he became more courageous and left the lines bare. I have seen many explanations of pictures by Picasso which ignore entirely things that I know were in his mind when he did them, but of which the commentators know nothing. This has mightily encouraged a skeptical trend in me regarding many matters which are plausibly explained to the satisfaction of those who must have an explanation, even when the explanation has no basis except the explainer's wish for an explanation.

In 1910 I bought my last picture from Picasso and that was one that I did not really want, but I had from time to time advanced him sums of money, and this cleared the account. Picasso was amusing sometimes when he was hard up. At one such moment the pictures of Renoir for the first time brought large prices at an auction, and Picasso, who had no coal and no money to buy it, drew glowing pictures of Renoir's house with sacks of coal everywhere and some specially choice hunks on the mantelpiece. Once when I gave him a hundred francs to buy coal, he stopped on the way home and spent sixty of it for Negro sculpture.

Picasso was not pleased that I would have none of his cubism. As long as he was not committed, but only experimenting, all went well enough between us, but when he had finally made the turning there was nothing to go on. Nonetheless, whenever we met he would recur to this and say, "Why don't you like my painting?" I explained over and over again, but he was not satisfied. Once he was angry and burst out, "You have no right to judge. I'm an artist, and you are not."

"But Pablo," I answered, "I deliberately and consciously avoid this subject. It's you who always raise it. Leave it alone, and nothing will be said about it."

When it happened that in order to buy a Renoir, I had

to sell some of his pictures, I asked Gertrude to let him know at once of my intention. He took it nicely and said, "If Leo sells pictures of mine to get a Renoir, I hope he'll get a good one." After I had the picture, I once saw him coming in to see Gertrude and I said, "Don't you want to see your Renoir?" He found it very good, and we had a pleasant talk. We went over the whole subject of his painting once more, and he concluded, "Even if this new way is a mistake, it has profited me, for I did a figure the other day and it was better than any I had done before." Soon after this I left Paris to live in Settignano, and I did not see Picasso again till after the war.

In 1920 I called on him at the Rue de la Boetie. He was a little bitter and not very polite. He said, "The trouble with you is that you can't see things till the cogs have become somewhat rusty." I didn't find this remark very clever. I had recognized the value of Picasso the first time I saw his work, and for a while was the only person that bought his pictures. I was the only person anywhere, so far as I know, who in those early days recognized Picasso *and* Matisse. Picasso had some admirers, and Matisse had some, but I was alone in recognizing these two as the two important men. Nor did I come to an admiration of cubism when the cogs had grown rusty. No, Picasso's comment, if it did not flatter me, did not flatter his judgment.

My interest in Picasso *and* Matisse calls to mind "kinds of things." Most people in matters of art are interested in some kind of thing, and are not interested in some other kind till it becomes a matter of habit. This habituation makes it possible to gather heterogeneous collections of the things that have been established, but for the new it's first a matter of kinds. That means that most people find it natural to belong to a sect, except for the few who find it equally natural to refuse to belong to a sect. I was never of either kind, but tended rather to consider the particular thing than the kind of thing that it was.

When I was fourteen I belonged to a baseball club, and was continually puzzled by the lack of objective vision of its members and those of other clubs with which we played. I couldn't understand how they could always see things in a purely partisan spirit. If it was a question of a foul or a pickup, those who saw the play and those who had their backs turned were equally sure and equally vociferous. I was the only one affected by what was actually seen. It has remained so ever since in art and other things. I am typically and essentially non-partisan and find myself under no spiritual necessity to be for or against anything. Therefore, it was easy enough to see that here were two great talents doing two entirely different things. One stuck to his line and has brought it far. The other had not sufficient character for this, and became the playboy of modern art. His emotional intensity is real, and he seems to be ending as he began—a great illustrator—and so he will have justified his talent.

The next time I saw Picasso was some years later when I met him on the street. I said, "You're getting fat."

"Yes," he said, patting his belly. "Isn't it shameful? I hear you're painting again."

"Yes."

"I'm curious to see what you're doing. Aren't you going to exhibit?"

"Not yet."

"Perhaps you're waiting till the crisis is over." This was after '29.

"I think I'd better," I replied.

"By the way, I saw Gertrude recently. She said to me, 'There are two geniuses in art today, you in painting and I in literature.' " Picasso shrugged his shoulders. "What do I know about it? I can't read English. What does she write?"

I said she used words cubistically, and that most people couldn't understand at all.

"That sounds rather silly to me. With lines and colors, one can make patterns, but if one doesn't use words according to their meanings, they aren't words at all."

"Well," I said, "if you want to know more about it, you'll have to ask someone more cubistically inclined than I am."

One more meeting, and that was the last. I happened in at Rosenberg's where some Picasso pictures were on exhibition, including the big *Dance*. Picasso came in and spoke to me a moment, but seemed nervous. "You look at the pictures," he said. "I'm going upstairs to smoke a cigarette. I'll be down soon." Picasso, I recognized, had now come into the class of Great Men, and as Emerson said after his visit to England in '33, one talks to great men as one does to children, one humors them. So when he came down, I said that the action of the big *Dance* was splendid, which it is, and then we agreed in criticism of pictures by Leger which were also being shown, and everything went very nicely.

I am sorry that I did not see his *Guernica*. I returned from America while the World's Fair was still on, but the Spanish house was closed. From the photographs, one gets an impression of effectively applied expressive power. Of course, one cannot judge a big picture from a little reproduction, which often flatters it, but I certainly would like to see it.

As an appendix to this account of Picasso, I must say something about the Rousseau Banquet. Everyone who writes about those times gets round to it somehow. It has been overdescribed, and I don't propose to describe it again. I shall only tell how there came to be a banquet at all, for I was innocently the cause of it.

One day I had gone to see Picasso, who was not at home. While I was talking with Fernande, Rousseau came in to rest a moment, for he had been giving a violin lesson in the neighboring Rue Lepic. As I had never heard him, I asked him to play, but he excused himself: he was tired, and the day was hot. Then Fernande said, "Monsieur Rousseau, you must come to dinner soon and play for us and a few friends." Rousseau said he would be delighted, whereon Fernande added, "Let's not leave it at some time; make it a week from Saturday, and I'll ask the Steins, and Braque and Apollinaire and Marie Laurencin." That was agreed to, but when the news got about, so many others wanted to come that the dinner was changed to a picnic supper, famous through all the world as the Banquet Rousseau. Great oaks from little acorns grow. If I had not that drowsy summer afternoon asked Rousseau to play, there would have been no banquet, and no post-fabricated explanations to account for it.

Matisse's work, unlike Picasso's, was one whose genuineness one could never question. He played with cubism a little and profited by Negro sculpture, but he was too intelligent and too sincere to drown in these things. He experimented, but kept control. One summer he brought back from the country a study of a young fisherman, and also a free copy of it with extreme deformations. At first he pretended that this had been made by the letter-carrier of Collioure, but finally admitted that it was an experiment of his own. It was the first thing he did with forced deformations. He also brought back some landscapes in bright colors, which at first attracted me so strongly that I wanted the whole lot; but I could only get two of them, as the others were already promised. In these, for the first time, I noticed that after a little while the essential rhythm went flat. However, despite this, what he did always interested me, and I was always wanting to see what he did next. One could be certain that he was properly carrying on.

I thoroughly understood his work, and this he then recognized. One day he came to the house to ask me to do something. He was always diffident when asking, and it took some time for him to get to the point. Young men, office workers and others, had formed a group to visit the ateliers of painters, where someone would make a little speech about their work. He wanted me to make this speech for him. I declined. I said that I was ready to talk French extemporaneously, but not to address Frenchmen deliberately in their own tongue. Matisse urged me, as he said there was no one else to do it, but I had to refuse. I mention it as evidence from Matisse himself that I really understood him.

While on this theme, I can tell a characteristic Vollard incident. In the earliest days, I once talked to Vollard for a long time about Matisse. Vollard listened intently, and when I concluded, he said, "And you really think that Matisse is as important as that?" I said that I did. This was in the early autumn, and we were expecting Matisse back from the country to show us his work first. He then said he had been much surprised to get a letter from Vollard, asking to see his pictures before they were offered to another dealer—since Vollard had never felt great interest in what he did. So I told him of this conversation, which made everything clear.

Vollard on another occasion was very Vollardian. He talked to me one day of the charms of Parisian society, and how I greatly erred in not getting out into that world. He expatiated on the conversation of the French salons, in which I should take a part. I assured him that this sort of thing was not at all in my line, and quite out of the question, but I was surprised by his speaking of it. Meeting Picasso the next day, I told him about this strange attack. Picasso laughed. Yes, he said, Vollard had already spoken to him of this, and what splendid publicity I could supply if I would go out into society and talk about painting. In fact, however, I confined myself to 27 Rue de Fleurus, which will be the subject of the next chapter.

VIII

27 Rue de Fleurus

27 RUE DE FLEURUS was filling with pictures, and also with visitors. My brother, who was our banker, surprised me one day when he said we had eight thousand unexpended francs. As this was regarded as criminal waste, we went at once to Vollard's. Vollard liked to sell us pictures because, as he told me, we were the only customers who bought pictures, not because they were rich, but despite the fact that they weren't. So we never had to bargain with him, as he always gave us good prices. Besides, he said, the rich paid when they happened to think of it, and their thoughts ran mostly to other matters, while we paid at once. On this occasion I selected two Gauguins, two

Cézanne figure compositions, two Renoirs, and Vollard threw in a Maurice Denis, *Virgin and Child*, for good measure. In later years, people often said to me that they wished they were able to buy such things for such prices, and I had to remind them that they also were in Paris then and had more money than I had. But they, to use Picasso's words, had to wait till the cogs were rusty, or—as it would perhaps be better to say—till they were worn smooth and ran easily.

One day at the Autumn Salon I had picked out some pictures to buy—a Bonnard, a Vuillard and something else—but when I came to the office it was closed. So I went to lunch, intending to finish the affair later. But while eating, I got an idea that was thrilling: to buy a big Cézanne figure, instead of a lot of little pictures. Vollard was enthusiastic, and wanted us to have the largest possible range of choice. He would say, "Wait, I can get some other ones to show you," and so for several weeks we toddled over to the Rue Lafitte again and again. It was difficult to make a choice, because all these pictures are fragmentary and unfinished, and each has in it good and bad. One had to compromise, unless one was rich enough to buy half a dozen of them and have the pictures supplement each other.

Our collection became in time one of the sights of Paris, for everyone who was curious to know modern art. We were supposed by many to be eccentric millionaires who wore corduroys and lived in a pavilion—that is, a little detached house in a court—in order to be different. A bearded porter at the Gare St. Lazare came to me once when I was leaving after having seen a friend off, and asked me about my philosophy of life. Just then my beard was bushy because, as often, I had forgot to get it trimmed, and I wore sandals and corduroys. I was surprised, and said that I had no particular philosophy of life. But I must have, he insisted: when cultured people do things different from those done by others, it must be because they have a philosophy of life. So I told him that I was both disorderly and careless, and sometimes I forgot to shave. I didn't like finding myself, suddenly, unshaved, and so I grew a beard. As for the sandals, I had once worn them all the summer, and on my return to the city my feet were blistered when I took a long walk, and so I came back to the sandals. The corduroys were convenient, for they were not made of wool, and so there was no need of precautions to keep the moths off. The disappointed porter turned away. I ought to have asked him for his philosophy of life, for certainly he had one.

Sometimes people who knew our circumstances wanted to know how we managed. We not only had the pictures, but also thousands of books; we traveled as we wanted to and entertained a great deal. The only explanation I could give was that we never kept any accounts and never had any debts. The dealers often wanted to sell me things which I could pay for later, but I would have none of this. We spent all the money we had and no more, and so we were free. Life was then cheap in Paris, rents were low, food was not dear, we had no doctor's bills. There were good little restaurants wherever one traveled, and we didn't expect hot and cold running water in the hotels we stopped at—or any running water, for that matter. We despised luxury except when someone else paid for it, and got what we most wanted. That made a satisfactory living.

Our collection was not a collection of specimens, and many well-known painters were not represented. There was no Derain. In an early Autumn Salon I noticed an *Interior* that seemed good to me. The price was only a hundred francs, but I never liked to buy pictures by unknown men till I had seen them at least twice, for then one incurs a responsibility, as when one does a favor of which a repetition is expected. This picture of Derain's on a second view was not good enough. So it always remained, they were never good enough, and I never bought any. He had a curious way of painting a head as though this was cut off from a large figure, and of putting a figure into a place where it did not fit—a curious and unique perversity. His most satisfying pictures were his russet still lifes, but even these I did not care to have.

Though Braque was for some time one of the intimates at the house, I never had anything of his. His precubist paintings were insignificant, and the earlier cubist things were like Picasso's, but weaker. His little dark decorative still lifes were the first interesting things he did, and by that time I was no longer actively concerned with pictures.

Of Van Gogh I never had anything, and I would rather read his letters than look at his pictures. Van Gogh was sensitive, appreciative to an unusual degree, intelligent, and keenly interested, but he had hardly, as he himself said, finished his apprenticeship, before he went mad. Once Fenéon, when he was in charge of the modern pictures at Bernheim's, was unpacking a large consignment of

Van Goghs as I happened in. We looked over them together. When he asked me what I thought of them, I said that if these had been by Cézanne or Matisse, they would have held them to be interesting beginnings, though it still remained to make pictures of them. That is the way with most of his work. However profound they may be emotionally, they are pictorially too superficial to amount to much. They are mostly intense impressions. He had worked so long and seriously at composition that these impressions had often a real formal intention which was incompletely realized. His earlier things that were more thoroughly worked are student's work. On the whole I prefer his drawings, especially his landscape drawings, to his paintings.

We had an exquisite little Manet and a little head by Daumier. There was a Greco *St. Francis* that came from South America, and a Delacroix. It is long since Delacroix has been the fashion, but I consider him to be by all odds the greatest French painter of his century. It has always amused me that the people who say that the subject does not count object to Delacroix's romantic subjects. If the subject makes no difference, why should one object to "Brian de Bois Guilbert carrying off Rebecca from the burning castle of Front de Boeuf?" The important question is, can the painter get away with it, and Delacroix could. He was one of the rare dramatic artists who is a real painter—one with Giotto, Michelangelo, Tintoretto, Rubens—a great colorist, a great master. It has become one of the conventions of our day that a picture is primarily, and then exclusively, a matter of paint, but that this should be so is not at all obvious. In fact, it was obvious until quite recently that pictures should say things of interest, and that the art of painting was to say them well. There came about a period in painting when the academician was dominant, and the specific art was neglected, but even then it was possible to make pictures that were good as illustration and of permanent interest, if one had a sufficient dramatic gift.

Jean Paul Laurens was one who had this gift. I once asked a superior person whether he remembered a certain picture by Laurens in the Luxembourg. He snorted indignation at the suggestion that he should remember a Laurens, but when I began to describe the picture, he knew it well. As painting, it was not good, but as with color one can legitimately do anything that color will do, and as drama is one of those things, such pictures are entirely reputable. I would rather have a good Laurens or a good Meissonier than half a ton of the empty canvases covered moderately well with paint that of late years one has seen everywhere. People have a very mistaken notion that their conventions are something more than conventions. It is not a convention to say that Laurens is not a great "painter," but it is a convention to say that what he does well is unimportant. There are not as yet ascertained laws of nature which tell what it is in art that shall be considered important. This still remains a matter of opinion.

The bulk of the collection at 27 Rue de Fleurus was made of Picassos, Matisses, Cézannes and Renoirs. I noticed once that when I hung all the Renoirs together they enhanced each other, but grouping the Cézannes had no such result. Another thing I noticed was that when I returned from Italy at the end of the summer, the Cézannes maintained their full affirmations, but all the other things were somewhat dimmed and needed a little time to recover. I did not then have a fully developed late Renoir or Matisse, but nonetheless the fact was interesting.

The Saturday evenings became more and more crowded. I expounded and explained. Some people are given to explaining. I knew an Englishman in Florence, a mere acquaintance whom I saw at times in a *caffé* or, more commonly, on a street corner. Once I came upon him in the Piazza Santa Trinita and he told me that he had bought an apartment, that he had tried several towns but had come back to Florence, which he preferred. He didn't know why, because he thought he liked some others better. So I explained to him why he preferred Florence.

"There it is," he said, "my wife and I were talking about this, and I said to her that when I met Mr. Stein I'd bring up the subject and that he would explain it—and so you have."

Professor Boas of Johns Hopkins University once said to me that if he knew ever so little about a subject he could get up on a platform and give an hour's lecture on it. I can't give a lecture, but I can explain. So on Saturday evenings I explained. One young fellow who greatly admired a Greco-Romantic painter named Ménard came one evening and, when leaving, said, "Oh, I'll admit that you can talk, but that doesn't alter the facts." There are people whose confidence in the facts is proof against all attack.

A year later he came again. He said, "You don't remember me."

I said, "Oh, yes, how's Ménard?"

"Rotten," said he, and after that came almost every Saturday.

At the beginning, some of my friends who thought a strayed sheep like myself ought to be brought back to the flock, decided that one of them should speak seriously to me about my blunders, but Bancel La Farge told me that no one would take on the role of bell-the-cat. So I was left to go on, and in time most of them were following.

There was an Englishman who came one evening and grew indignant. "Why do you just sit there and talk to these docile people?" he stormed. "Why don't you go out and encounter those who disagree and are competent to maintain their disagreement?"

I said that I had no program, but acted quite casually. People came, and so I explained, because it was my nature to explain. Many wanted to know why I didn't write. I said I couldn't write. This was before I knew of Freud, so I could not tell them about inhibitions. If I had been living somewhere else, I would have known about Freud before this, but he was late to arrive in France. So I talked, and some of what I said got into books without my putting pen to paper. Eventually I tried psychoanalysis, but as that did not work, I developed a method for myself that did work. Then I wrote some articles; when I had analyzed some more I wrote a book; and now that my analysis is unusually complete, it looks as though I would do nothing else but write and paint.

When my interest in Cézanne declined, when Matisse was temporarily in eclipse, when Picasso turned to foolishness, I began to withdraw from the Saturday evenings. After a time the pictures which were joint property of Gertrude and myself were divided, and I exchanged many for Renoirs. The Gauguins I had long before disposed of.

Gauguin made an important departure, but he is only second-rate. I don't want any pictures in my room that I could not recommend for the Louvre—except my own. I can have these around because I can consider their defects with a remunerated eye, as I think how to make them better. For those of others, I can only regret that they did not do this, and sometimes a specific defect becomes so annoying that the picture has to be done away with. A picture may have many deficiencies and yet be tolerable, while some apparently trifling misadventure in composition may disrupt the whole.

In "modern art" I was never interested. I don't even know what it is, and I dislike the term. If the phrase meant anything important, it would mean art produced by a modern mind. Obviously not Cézanne or Renoir or Matisse or Picasso—though he is now a communist—is a modern mind. I shan't discuss the matter here, as I propose to write a book about the modern mind, which really does not yet exist. The mind of today is the same old mind as ever, though it has a greater interest in gadgets. I think it is better to say recent art, or contemporary art. Much of this contemporary art is "abstract," and therefore something must be said of this.

Distortion in art has already been spoken of. It is found everywhere, since anything which is seen out of focus is of necessity distorted, and everything particular in a work of art is out of focus, since it is seen as related to something not itself. In recent years distortion has come to be cherished. Cézanne distorted noticeably—not because he wanted to, but because only so could he get his results. Matisse distorted more than he wished to distort. At the time when his distortions were most extreme and offensive to the general, he told me that at every beginning of a picture he hoped that he could end without any distortion that would offend the public, but that he could not succeed. In his popular Nice period he did succeed, and much of his distortion since is not of the pseudo-naturalistic kind, but decorative.

Much of Picasso's distortion in the Negroid period was a facile means for securing tension in drawing, which he lacked. Sometimes he put the lower half of a face at an angle to the upper half, instead of subtly modifying the curvature. Modigliani also makes things easier by distortion. His best things are admirably harmonized and rhythmed; and this can, of course, be more easily done when heads and necks, and torsos and limbs, can be given arbitrary proportions. The result, to my thinking, is rather offensive. It is more or less ugly—that is, not what we expect in a face or figure that is not purposely caricatured. All essential values can be achieved without these manifest distortions, but it is not so easy; and Modigliani, like so many others of today, thinking ugliness a virtue, preferred the easier way.

Abstract art was bound to come to people's minds after Cézanne, even though Cézanne's painting was not so different from what had gone before as theorists often pretend. There is distortion in all art, but obvious distortion in former art had been interpretive, a fashion in shapes, and so intentional, or else it was caricature, while Cézanne's was compositional and so incidental. This implied that the subject might fairly be subordinated to the purpose of the picture as a whole. Courbet had already given the shove toward any subject being good enough, and so one was launched toward the objective that no-subject would serve one's purpose. A great deal has been written about abstract art, and of this I have seen very little. Also there are many painters of abstract pictures whose works I have not seen. What I have to say is not grounded in a scholarly acquaintance with the subject, and is justified perhaps only because these chapters are autobiographical.

Abstraction in art may mean two very different things —abstraction of qualities and abstraction of subject matter. Abstraction of qualities is essentially a matter of attention, of direction of interest. One person may be interested most in form, another in drama, another in social significance, another in philosophy or religion, and so on. This kind of abstraction can never be delivered pure, since it is in its nature interpretive and there must be something to interpret. It is the abstraction of subject matter which has had a recent emergence.

The thing is not entirely new. Reynolds believed that draperies should be abstract in so far as they should not be woolen or cotton or silk, but just draperies. Picasso went further. A nose should not be a Greek nose or a Roman nose or a snub nose—in short not *a* nose but *the* nose. Finally a nose need not even be a nose at all, but anything else, or almost nothing at all. By that time a nose had reached the limit of abstraction. This was one way to become abstract.

Abstraction could be come to by other roads. One might condense one's feelings into form. There were horizontality and verticality and obliquity, there were feelings of heat and cold, of sublimity and the trivial, and there were lines and squares and circles and spirals, and hot and cold colors.

With these one could say all that one wanted, without the horizontals being fields, the verticals trees, the obliques perspectives, or the colors being the colors of objects. Inevitably people tried out this sort of thing and got some results. Some find the results satisfying, and some do not. I am one of those who is only a little thrilled.

There are some persons who think that, apart from its results in practice, the idea of abstract art is important. I am one of those who thinks that ideas in art may be amusing and sometimes serviceable, but that they are never important. I do not mean that they may not be important for the artist. Picasso had ideas that I consider silly, and yet they made a great difference to him and to subsequent art. What I mean is that the work of art stands on its own bottom, and is made neither better nor worse because of intentions in the artist's mind. Reynolds may have thought that while a mere man may look well dressed in a silk gown, a hero is rightly garbed only in neutral stuff. A hero may be considered a sort of abstraction, and should be abstractly clothed. Picasso thought it a fault that Cézanne and Renoir made use of real noses, when in truth only unreal noses were really real. Even when reasons are as plentiful as blackberries, one should be careful about using them, since they are often either unripe or rotten.

I shall consider one case where the thesis of abstract art is developed with Cézanne as its object—not what Cézanne painted, but what he is interpreted as thinking. I have seen a good many of these profound lucubrations in notices of pictures and reviews of books. I have no American books at hand, and shall use an English one, *Art Now,* by Herbert Read. Read is said to be the leading English critic of this stripe, so the examination is not unfair.

Though Read's objective is Cézanne, he starts far back with Plato. Plato in the *Philebus* discusses kinds of pleasure, and comes to a pleasure in what he calls pure beauty. "I do not intend by beauty of shapes what most people would expect, such as that of living creatures or pictures, but for the purpose of my argument, I mean straight lines and curves and the surfaces or solid forms produced out of these by lathes and rulers and squares." To make the matter clearer, he adds, "Such sounds as are pure and smooth and yield a single pure tone," and a little further along—this Read does not quote—"Then we shall be perfectly right in saying that a little pure white is whiter and more beautiful and truer than a great deal of mixed white." Read concludes, "The *Philebus* is Plato's last work, and here we have a definite abandonment of the unfortunate theory of *mimesis,* or art conceived as a technique for the direct imitation of the appearance of things."

In short, when Plato says precisely that he is not referring to art, that is, to pictures, but to a certain kind of pleasure which he calls the pleasure in absolute beauty, and according to which pure white is more beautiful and *truer* than gray, Read says he is offering a theory of art; though anyone who wanted this pure white would ask a chemist to make it and not an artist.

When someone who ought to know what he is talking about talks what seems to be nonsense, one tries to find sense in it somehow, but here I can find none whatever. Still less, if possible, when Read goes on to Cézanne. Plato's remark about the forms made with lathes and rulers and squares, Read says, comes very near to Cézanne's words regarding spheres, cones and cylinders. Here nonsense, to my thinking, becomes sheer extravagance. I have never seen one bit of evidence to show that Cézanne, when he referred to these geometric forms, meant anything else than what drawing teachers who refer to them have meant: that a head is essentially a sphere, the trunk and limbs essentially cylinders and cones, and that it is bad academic drawing to ignore these underlying forms. Cézanne was insisting on a commonplace—which does not mean that he was being commonplace, since commonplaces are often very much to the point. Cézanne told Vollard that he should pose like an apple: does an apple budge? Of course an apple budges if you give it time enough. It shrivels, discolors, rots.

If Cézanne had wanted to paint spheres and cylinders and cones, he would have done so, and he could have had them made of good hard wood, and they would not have budged in forty years. There is no evidence that he had anything of the sort in his mind, and there is much evidence that he didn't. Cézanne was what few good painters are, an intellectual, and he thought clearly and expressed himself precisely. Read speaks of his "innocent way" in saying that he wanted to do Poussin again after nature, and to make of impressionism something solid and enduring like the art in the museums; but these remarks are not "innocent." They say exactly what he meant. Plato, who was a philosopher and psychologist, also said exactly what he meant, and he did not mean at all the same thing as Cézanne, who talked not as a philosopher or psychologist, but as a painter.

There has been in recent years a large output of abstract

art, of which I have seen very little. Of what I know, either in originals or reproduction, that which pleased me most was Calder's, Mondrian's and Paul Klee's. Calder's contraptions are so lively, so alert, that I was always entertained. They gave an impression of fullness of form, and have the great advantage that they wiggle. Klee is the only abstractionist whose work is sensitive enough to be charming. Mondrian avoids confusion, is exquisite in his sense of measure, and is the extreme opposite to Calder—the absolute no-wiggle contrasted with the wiggle. Other than these, what I have seen has left me indifferent. I am not prejudiced against it, but I don't find that it satisfies enough to be bothered with.

Western man is a restless animal, and the creative spirit is the spirit of restlessness. Many who are thus restless, and who cannot create, are eager to follow the latest novelty—which, of course, is not always an advance. The conservative does not approve. He thinks that when you have something good, you had better stick to it. The Athenian in Plato's *Laws* says that in Egypt, "You will find that their works of art are painted and moulded in the same forms which they had ten thousand years ago."

"How extraordinary."

"I should rather say how statesmanlike, how worthy of a legislator."

True, if one had once discovered the perfect world, it might be well to take up within it one's permanent habitation, but as yet this is to seek. We prefer when we have been roasted long enough on one side to turn the other, especially if we are artists, and it is not in the cards that this process will soon be arrested.

IX

Appreciation and Education

THERE is self-education and education by others. There is education that is intended, and education that just happens. But of necessity there is either education or stagnation.

There is education of the body and education of the mind. This is not as simple as it sounds, for there is an education of the body that is not physical education. For purposes of science it is probably enough to use the mind. The facts lie outside us and need to be related and re-related; ideas connect them; and so things go onward. The genius of discovery is more profound, but nonetheless, important acquisitions can be made on the cerebral level. But for appreciations to be effective, something more than this is needed. These involve more amply the so-called emotions, which are more corporeal and less exclusively cerebral than what is employed in mere knowing.

In the discussions that I have noted taking place in America today, there is constant recurrence of the terms, liberal education, classical education, education through the Great Books, and so on. I think another and more vital classification would be serviceable, and though the subject is much too large for a concluding chapter, it fits well enough into this book to be at least referred to.

Education, as I see it, can be for three things mainly—intellectual education, learning to understand and manipulate ideas; practical education, learning to manipulate instruments and materials; education for appreciation. There is also an education of a lower order, which is education for routine and is better called training. This is applied to animals as well as human beings. It is the method of dogma, of the ten commandments. Thou shalt not steal: that is, thou shalt not take what does not belong to thee. But the subtly complex question of what should be yours and what another's is not gone into.

It is possible to consider morals in another way, to consider them in terms of appreciations. Thou shalt love thy neighbor as thyself. Obviously I can't if I don't like him, and I can't like him if I don't appreciate him. Even if I do, I mightn't like him; but if we appreciate each other, things would be more promising. Appreciation is a basic concept for many things.

Far too much fuss is made about art, as though it were important because it is art. Art merely as art is an amusement, and nothing more. Art for art's sake is a silly slogan, as though one ought to be a high-stepper and go prancing along, admiring the perfection of one's gait. There is nothing discreditable about this; it is a quite decent way of amusing oneself. But art is important only as an integral part of culture, and that concerns appreciations of all kinds.

One can hardly speak of education today without regard to what the world promises and threatens. The atomic bomb has put its thunderous emphasis on the fact that the culture of the past is not good enough. The fatuous persons who see in Greece or the thirteenth century a model for the modern world have only to consider how pleased the Athenians or the Popes would have been if they had possessed a medium like the bomb to compel the whole world to their orders. They used whatever they had, though that was not enough. People today are as like as two peas to what people were then, though the conditions were different. The Greeks were not a people specially devoted to art, but to politics. The people of the Middle Ages were more credulous than we are, and therefore more religious, as credulous people universally are.

It is not really difficult to understand the past if we remember the simple fact that the differences between us and them are differences of condition. We ignore the conditions and try to imagine some other kind of people. Of course it is difficult to know enough of any special situation to be sure of understanding it, but that applies also to yesterday and today in our own country. In the last few years American history has been entirely rewritten, and the rewriting continues. The minds of other times concerned themselves with interests then dominant, but those interests are almost always interests that in us too could be awakened if the conditions demanded it. Everyone is superstitious enough, is avaricious enough, is indifferent enough or cruel enough, to understand the extremes of these things in others, if he really let himself appreciate himself. But when we read history, we try to understand it outside ourselves, and in consequence it is something in which all the actors are other kinds.

"Look in thy heart and write," said Sir Philip Sidney. For intellectual and practical education, this is not necessary; for everything else it is. It is, however, not our way to know much of ourselves except distantly, and so we understand very little of what can be understood in no other way. We take ourselves for granted, and because Freud has revealed the unconscious, a lot of silly people think there is some special merit in recording what comes out of these opened sores. They create works of art that are as meritorious as the mechanical outpourings of Goldberg. Others imagine that the Great Books are magical transformers, regardless of what the world has been for centuries, with and without the great books. Triviality is the dominant note in all these discussions.

The great plaint of the times is that science outruns humanity. Of course. Science is what could have been done by the people of any time if the necessary conditions had existed; that is, the persons themselves need not have been changed, but the ability to make a better use of science means a change in those who use it. For this there was formerly no technique available except religion. A few people here and there were permanently converted, but only on condition that they profoundly believed things that were perhaps, or even probably, not true. A new world can date only from Freud—not that he brought it in, but that he did for appreciation what Galileo did for knowing; he unlocked the door. We must become capable of change without first drowning in credulity, and must not be content with programs for changing others. Everyone who wishes to practice psychoanalysis must first be analyzed, but for the most part this amounts to little more than getting a little insight into himself. Much more than this is prospectively necessary.

It has long been evident that modern knowledge is inconsistent with the competitive system, and the atomic bomb now dots the i's and crosses the t's, but people as they are cannot be socialists. They can read novels and treatises on the subject, and consider pros and cons, but they cannot be it or even realize what it means. To "appreciate" in a book a thing that one cannot appreciate in real life, is ivory tower appreciation. Every intelligent person can see this in Abie and his Irish Rose, but not when presented at a higher level. Both are forms of escape. The philosophically-minded who have a new philosophy every ten years are just clowning with philosophy. They feel deeply with Bergson one day, with Husserl another day and just now it's Kierkegaard. Does this change them? Not a bit. They are simply having fun with a new dialect. The critic I quoted as saying that Picasso could give fresh charm to the "neo-classic" was talking about words, not things. So it is for the most part. We are really at too grave a moment in the course of events to admit that our teachers are competent to teach. *Quis custodiet istos custodes?*

The concluding chapter of this book is not the place to go into this matter more deeply or more extensively. The chief value of the study of history is to show that people in the historic period have always been the same, but that what they know has altered their ways. Chance just put into my hands *The Psychological Frontiers of Society* by Kardiner, which in this professionally confirms my amateur opinion. Now the time has come when the need of altering their ways is so great that they themselves must be altered. Hitherto the function of knowledge has been to change the machine, and to play at improving the machinist. Psychology must learn to do something better than improving the methods of gulling people by advertisements or dividing the sheep from the goats for some practical purpose. It has, to be sure, helped the neurotics. It must now help to save the world from the far more dangerous "normal" people. Even a Hitler could not have done much more than make a noise without the efficient help of the "perfectly sane." For many years to come, we must remain at the mercy of big business men, senators, diplomats, clergymen, professors and the rest. Perhaps the bomb will get its innings first, perhaps not. Who lives, will see.

The concept of appreciation is, I believe, a useful and unifying one. It applies to the whole realm of things that can't be counted, can't be measured, can't be analyzed other than roughly—the things that, to be of great importance, have to be taken into our psychophysical organism as a whole. The long duration of analyses in psychiatry is due to the ineffectualness of knowledge to change personality. Sometimes in the process of analysis forgotten events are recalled, but for the most part the patient knows all that is necessary, though he takes good care that it does not get to be so deeply known as to make any effective difference. As soon as the knowledge threatens his organism as a whole, he shuts it off and perhaps takes a little illness on the side. Only the attrition of repetition on repetition wears down the resistance. One can't have everything, and for a long time a mere disturbance of one's health seems a small price to pay for the privilege of remaining profoundly and terribly a fool.

Wisdom is a good for which some sacrifices may well be made. But wisdom that is worth having must be brought down to earth. It must not remain unused, unutilizable speculation, mere ritual of thinking. To bring it to earth is a long and tedious matter, demanding sacrifices of those who would make it serviceable. Wisdom flies on eagle wings through the air, but on the solid earth a snail's pace is the measure of its progress.

Index

95430
E9-Sonet